How the

FENDER BASS

Changed the World

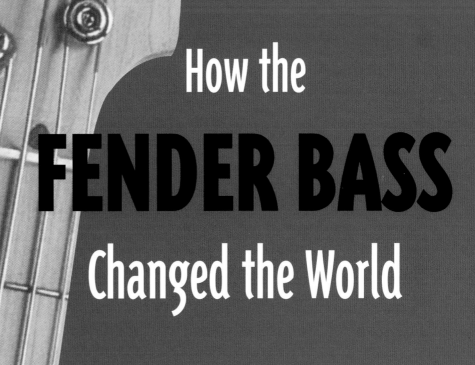

How the
FENDER BASS
Changed the World

By Jim Roberts

Backbeat
Books

San Francisco

Published by Backbeat Books
600 Harrison Street
San Francisco, CA 94107
www.backbeatbooks.com
Email: books@musicplayer.com
An imprint of Music Player Network
United Entertainment Media, Inc.
Publishers of *Bass Player* and MusicPlayer.com

Distributed to the book trade in the U.S. and Canada by
Publishers Group West, 1700 Fourth Street, Berkeley, CA 94710

Distributed to the music trade in the U.S. and Canada by
Hal Leonard Publishing, P.O. Box 13819, Milwaukee, WI 53213

Cover Design: Damien Castaneda

Cover Photos: 1953 Fender Precision Bass by John Peden
                Jaco Pastorius by Tom Copi
                John Entwistle by Len DeLessio
                Jack Bruce courtesy of Redferns
                James Jamerson by Jon Sievert

Text Design and Composition: Greene Design

Library of Congress Cataloging-in-Publication Data

Roberts, Jim (James H.)
  How the Fender bass changed the world / by Jim Roberts.
    p. cm.
  Includes bibliographical references and index.
  ISBN 0-87930-630-0 (alk. paper)
   1. Bass guitar--History. 2. Fender guitar--History. 3. Bass guitarists.
    I. Title.

ML1015.B35 R63 2001
787.87'19--dc21
                                        2001025381

01 02 03 04 05   5 4 3 2 1
Printed in China through Colorcraft Ltd., Hong Kong

Dedication

To James Jamerson,
who showed the world what could be done
with the Fender bass,
and Jack Bruce,
whose brilliant playing in Cream inspired me
to become a bass player.

Acknowledgments

The initial inspiration for this book came when Nicky Orta and Matt Bonelli invited me to give a lecture at their 1993 Jazz Bass Conference in Miami, Florida. Not knowing what to talk about, I began to consider the largely unchronicled history of the electric bass. The outline I developed for that lecture was later expanded in a series of *Bass Player* magazine columns published in 1998; they became the starting point for this book.

For the most part this is a book of analysis and opinion, not primary history, so I'm grateful to all of the writers whose hard work has contributed to my knowledge of musical instruments and the musicians who play them. They're all listed in Sources, but I owe special thanks to Chris Jisi, Richard R. Smith, Mikael Jansson, Allan Slutsky, and Tom Wheeler. Special thanks also to Christian Fabian, who contacted me with the story of Leo Fender's 1952 meeting with Lionel Hampton, and Dan Lakin of Lakland Basses, who heard me give a short talk about the electric bass at a trade-show event and said, "Hey, Jim, why don't you write a book?" And, of course, I owe a great deal to the staff of *Bass Player*, past and present, and to the folks at Backbeat Books, especially Matt Kelsey and Dorothy Cox.

As a bass historian, I must acknowledge all of the help I have gotten from my colleague Tony Bacon. We've swapped information about the electric bass for years, and our ongoing dialogue has greatly enhanced my understanding of the development of the instrument. We've also had some memorable Italian dinners together in the unlikely locale of Frankfurt, Germany. Tony is unfailingly witty and gracious, and I am indebted to him in many ways.

Many thanks to Tom Wheeler, Chris Jisi, and my wife, Susan Strahosky, for reading the manuscript and offering dozens of good suggestions for improving the material. I shudder to think what this book might have

■ Acknowledgments

been without their guidance. I'm also grateful to Richard Johnston, for being such a skillful and reasonable editor; to Paul Haggard, who was the best possible art director for the project; and to the production team at Backbeat Books that pulled everything together, especially Amanda Johnson and Gary Montalvo.

Most of all, I want to thank Susan and our children, Miles and Nadia, for showing a great deal of patience and understanding during the many evenings, weekends, and holidays when I was working on this book.

Table of Contents

Foreword by **Marcus Miller**

In 1971, the bass guitar was the coolest instrument in music. All the cool cats played one. Larry Graham played one with Sly & the Family Stone, and Jermaine Jackson played one with the Jackson 5. If you wanted to be cool like these cats, you played bass. One popular band even named themselves after their bass player. What was his name? "Kool," of course!

In the early and mid '70s, bands like Kool & the Gang, Sly & the Family Stone, and the Jackson 5 created music that set the world on fire—and every song had a sweet bass line that kept the music (and your head) bouncing. Isaac Hayes even revolutionized the cinematic world that year with his "Theme from Shaft," which had the coolest bass line ever.

As a 12-year-old in '71, I decided I had to play bass. My buddies Brian, Tony, and Ferg all decided the same thing: "We're gonna play bass!" We called it "bass," not "bass guitar," because—to be honest—we didn't know any other kind of bass existed. As long as we'd been aware of music (six or seven whole years!), the bass had been played on a bass guitar. Sure, we'd seen the acoustic bass standing in the orchestra room at school, but it never occurred to any of us that anybody really played that thing (except maybe Snoopy in the "Peanuts" cartoons!). No, for us 12-year-olds, "bass" meant "bass guitar," the coolest instrument in the band.

Little did we know that the instrument we were so drawn to was really a baby, not much older than us. It's amazing that in the short time between when the instrument first appeared on records in the early 1950s and when I decided to play it in 1971, the bass guitar literally took over. Yeah, the electric guitar turned a lot of heads in those same years, but the bass guitar was the instrument that let you know the '50s were over and music was going to some new places.

In this book, Jim Roberts tells the story of the electric bass guitar. After reading it, I felt fortunate to have been able to witness an instrument's coming of age. The '60s and '70s were amazing years for the bass guitar. It was a new instrument and there were no rules. The piano is, what, 300 years old? There aren't many new ways to play a piano. You might think you've discovered something new, but there's a good chance some Austrian cat figured it out on harpsichord a couple hundred years ago. But the bass guitar—it really was a new instrument. Cats were free to discover its possibilities. They strummed it, plucked it, thumped it—whatever. And the creative atmosphere of those times fueled their discoveries. What we have now, in the year 2001, is a mature instrument played by thousands of people all over the world.

Check out the story of the bass guitar, the coolest instrument in the band!

Leo Fender with the original Fender Precision Bass, introduced in 1951.

Overture

When radio repairman and inveterate tinkerer Leo Fender invented the instrument he called a Precision Bass, he had modest goals. As he later told Tom Wheeler: "We needed to free the bass player from the big dog-house, the acoustic bass. That thing was usually confined to the back of the band, and the bass player couldn't get up to the mike to sing. And...guitar players would have an advantage if they could have an instrument with frets that would make doubling on bass easier for them."

Leo Fender did not invent the electric bass. The credit for that goes to Lloyd Loar, who conceived of an amplified "stick" bass in the 1920s. Leo Fender did not even invent the electric bass guitar, although he has often been credited with doing so. It now seems clear that Paul Tutmarc had the idea first. Tutmarc designed and produced a horizontally played, fretted electric bass in the mid 1930s. His instrument did not gain much acceptance and soon disappeared from sight. (A Tutmarc bass is on display at the Experience Music Project museum in Seattle.)

What Leo Fender *did* do was invent the first commercially successful electric bass guitar, which was introduced in 1951. Its acceptance was by no means a sure thing. The history of music is littered with seemingly impressive new instruments that were either ignored or, at best, played for a short time before being discarded. (Remember the telharmonium? Neither does anybody else.) A few new inventions became popular and eventually changed the course of music—the pianoforte, for instance— but these have been the exceptions. Leo Fender's Precision Bass is, without question, one of these notable exceptions.

When I first started to gather material for this book, my working title was "How the Electric Bass Changed the World." But as I learned more about the instrument's history—and especially after I investigated the work of Loar and Tutmarc—I realized it was the *Fender* bass that had triggered the revolutionary changes I wanted to write about. I find this remarkable, and I doubt there has ever been another mass-production musical instrument that has had such a singular impact. So, to be accurate, I revised the title of the book.

I mention this, at least in part, to allay any suspicions that this is somehow an "endorsed" or "commissioned" work the Fender Musical Instruments Corporation asked me to write. Nothing could be further from the truth. Our relationship is one of journalist and subject (and also musician and instrument)—nothing more.

In addition, my definition of "Fender bass" goes beyond the instru-

The Fender factory in Fullerton, California, as it looked in 1952, shortly after the introduction of the Precision Bass.

ments made by the Fender company to include other basses Leo Fender designed. The most important of these is the Music Man StingRay Bass, which Leo created (with some help from Forrest White) in the 1970s, after he had sold the Fender company to CBS. Leo also designed some good basses at G&L, his last company, before his death in 1991. These "post-Fender Fender basses" represent a continuation of the legacy that began with the original Precision Bass.

Leo Fender's basses have had a powerful influence on both musicians and musical-instrument designers, and that influence continues to this day. Thus, this is a tale of both technological and musical developments, of instruments and players—and of the greater world around them. I have tried to show how all of this is connected, because I believe that focusing on either the instruments alone or the musicians who played them ultimately produces a distorted and incomplete picture.

As I write this, the Fender bass is about to celebrate its 50th anniversary. While its musical capabilities are generally accepted today, its role as a powerful agent of change has been largely overlooked. As much as any other modern instrument, the Fender bass transformed the sound of popular music—and, in doing so, had an effect that reverberated beyond the bounds of popular culture.

Chapter 1: Long Before Leo

We think of the bass guitar as a *new* instrument and the double bass (the upright acoustic bass) as an *old* one. That's certainly true if we consider the electric bass as the primary example of the bass guitar family. There were some antecedents, but the electric bass as we know it traces its direct lineage back to the Fender Precision Bass of 1951. It's a mere babe, as musical instruments go.

The upright—the double bass—has a history that stretches back more than 500 years. There is evidence of upright stringed bass instruments from the late 1400s, and the earliest known illustration dates to 1516. These early basses were members of the viol family. Viols have fretted fingerboards and bodies with sloping shoulders; violins, which came along a little later, are fretless and have a different body shape, with rounded shoulders. (The terminology used at the time can be somewhat confusing. For instance, the word *violone* sometimes refers specifically to a bass viol but was loosely applied to just about any stringed bass instrument.)

As noted, viols have frets. These are pieces of gut tied around the fingerboard at the lowest five to seven half-steps. Most of the early bass viols had six strings, so the true origin of the fretted 6-string bass can be traced back several centuries. (And you probably thought it was Anthony Jackson's idea.)

The early stringed basses came in all sizes, from ones so large they required two men to play them to chamber instruments not much bigger than a cello. Regardless of the instrument's size, finding adequate strings was a major problem. The oversize gut strings required to play low *E* were criticized for being slack and indistinct. The problem was even worse when the lowest string was tuned to *C*.

A bass viol from 1701. Notice that this beautiful 6-string instrument has frets, which were pieces of gut tied around the fingerboard to provide more precise intonation.

To overcome some of the problems poor strings cause, bass players used dozens of different tunings. We know that some of the early bass viols were tuned *GCFADG* while others were tuned *DGCEAD*. Tunings of 5-string instruments included the familiar *EADGC* as well as *FADGC*, *DADF#B*, *FADF#A*, and lots of others. Bach's music has markings for basses in several different tunings, including the *violone grosso* (tuned *CGDA* like a cello, but an octave lower) and the *contrabass da Gamba* (tuned either *DGCEAD* or *GCFADG*). When 3-string basses became popular in the eighteenth century, they were tuned *ADG*, *GDG*, *GDA*, or maybe even *CGC*. The 4-string tuned *EADG* did not become the standard orchestra bass until early in the twentieth century. There were many other tunings, some of them *scordatura*: temporary retunings of one or more strings to suit a particular piece of music—a technique that Michael Manring has recently explored on electric bass with high artistry.

Vertical vs. Horizontal

There's no doubt that the upright bass, as played in orchestras, jazz groups, bluegrass bands, rockabilly combos, and various other settings, is an old instrument. But consider this: the antecedents of the modern bass guitar may be even older.

To understand this, you have to accept this assumption: Stringed bass instruments can be divided into two general groups, *vertical* basses and *horizontal* basses. The upright acoustic bass is the leading example of a vertical bass. The electric bass guitar is a horizontal bass (unless it's being played by Bill Wyman or Fieldy), and there are other horizontal bass instruments, including acoustic bass guitars—and some very old forms of bass lutes.

The lute is an ancient instrument. There's evidence it existed in primitive form as far back as the ninth century, and it was at the height of its popularity in the sixteenth century, when the earliest bass viols were being built. Lutes and guitars have much in common, including a hollow body with a soundhole, a fretted fingerboard, and a peghead with tuning machines. The term *luthier*, now applied to guitar builders, originally referred to the makers of lutes. Even so, a lute is not a guitar—but it doesn't require a huge leap to think of the bass lutes of the Renaissance as forerunners of the modern bass guitar. It's also interesting to note that the lute was a vehicle for songs and other "popular music," and lute music was written in tablature—so the ancient lutenists might be thought of as the rock guitarists of their day.

In the middle of the sixteenth century, the desire for stronger bass accompaniment led to the development of bass instruments known as the *theorbo* and the *chitarrone*. These bass lutes had larger bodies and longer strings than standard lutes. As you can see in the photo on page 20, some of them had an extra set of bass strings, played open, that were attached to a separate peghead. On some "contrabass" chitarrones, these bass strings were more than five feet long. These huge lutes, it's safe to assume, must have sounded as impressive in the lower register as the bass viols of the day.

In his work *The Baroque Double Bass Violone*, musical historian Alfred Planyavsky cites a 1623 text that says: "The large body [of the theorbo] was fitted with two fingerboards in order to be able to be strung with double bass strings." This is a clear indication that the theorbo was capable of producing notes deep in the lower register and that it functioned as a bass, not baritone, instrument. Planyavsky's book draws from the work of seventeenth-century scholar Michael Praetorius, who frequently mentioned the theorbo and the chitarrone, spelling the latter *ghitaron*. This spelling suggests a kinship to the *guitarron*, the large acoustic bass guitar used in Mexican music. (*Chitarrone* is an Italian word; *Harper's Dictionary of Music* lists "bass guitar" as one of its meanings.)

In the baroque period (circa 1600–1750), the *basso continuo* (accompaniment indicated by bass notes only) of many pieces was provided by

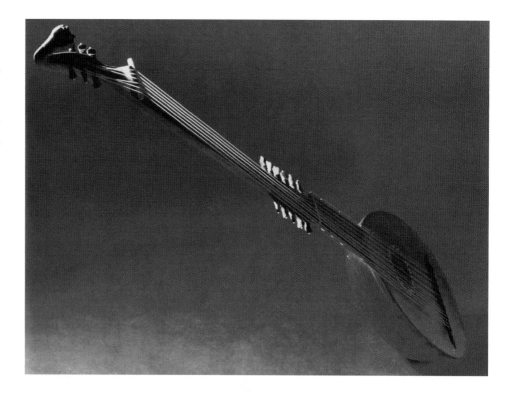

A seventeenth-century chitarrone. In many ways, this bass lute can be thought of as an ancestor of the modern bass guitar.

a trio often comprising a harpsichord, a theorbo, and a double bass. This pairing of two stringed bass instruments might be the earliest known example of "tic-tac" bass (see Chapter 6), with the bass lute providing punch while the bass viol, with its thick gut strings, filled out the bottom. The *basso continuo* "rhythm section" was a staple of musical performance well into the eighteenth century.

All of this suggests that the history of the bass guitar, if stretched to include other horizontal basses, goes back a lot further than we might have thought. We could even conclude that the horizontal and vertical approaches to building stringed bass instruments have developed in parallel over the past 500 years—so perhaps we should think of the double bass and the bass guitar as "cousins" rather than "father and son."

Attempts to build better upright acoustic basses and other types of acoustic bass instruments continued into the early twentieth century. But then a new factor entered the picture: electricity.

Chapter 2: Just Before Leo

Early in the twentieth century, mandolin orchestras sometimes included oversize "mando-basses" to provide the low end. These fretted instruments were usually played vertically, although this 1924 shot of the "Gibsonians" shows one in a semi-horizontal position with a special body support. (That's pioneering engineer Lloyd Loar on the far left.)

Volume is the problem. That's why stringed bass instruments have been made in so many different shapes and sizes: builders have been trying to make them louder. Instrument designers from the fifteenth century right up to today have experimented endlessly to build a bass that produced strong, clear, low-frequency sounds that projected well.

The first half of the twentieth century was a particularly fertile period for instrument development, and there were many attempts to build a better bass. One particularly loony idea was offered by a German inventor named Augustus Stroh, who created a whole line of mechanically amplified instruments. His bass had a solid body, with a bridge that rested on a flexible diaphragm. To the bridge he attached a large horn that looked like the ones found on early phonographs; the horn amplified the vibrations from the bridge, in the manner of a cheerleader's megaphone.

A more conventional approach to the volume problem involved taking an existing acoustic instrument and simply making it bigger: the

The Biggest Guitar In The World!

The
REGAL BASSOGUITAR

The BASSOGUITAR is just what the dance orchestra man or string band bass player is looking for.
This beautiful instrument combines the vast depth
and resonance of the double bass with the brilliant
tonal quality of the finest guitar! Strings and
tuning are the same as the double bass.

Novelty value of the BASSOGUITAR is very important. It is bound to be the talk of any night
club, tavern or stringed group . . . because it is the
biggest guitar in the world! It is a "Natural" for
small guitar groups using the double bass!

The BASSOGUITAR is played to best advantage by
slapping, plucking or picking (leather pick).

The BASSOGUITAR is a perfect instrument —
perfect in volume — in tone — and in attention
value!

BASSOGUITAR STRONGLY BUILT.
The BASSOGUITAR is strongly built, so that it can
stand up under the strain of constant travel.

Each $75.00
Mackintosh Cover—Snap Buttons 9.00
Covert Cover—Leather trimmed
   Slide Fastener 15.00

[38]

The Regal Bassoguitar of the 1930s was conceived as a cross between an acoustic guitar and an upright bass, as the company's sales literature made clear: "This beautiful instrument combines the vast depth and resonance of the double bass with the brilliant tonal quality of the finest guitar!"

"mando-bass," for example, was the largest member of the mandolin family. Gibson, Vega, and other manufacturers offered these fretted bass instruments, which supplied the low end in the mandolin orchestras that were popular in the early 1900s.

One of the most interesting instruments in this respect was the Regal Bassoguitar. Introduced in the early 1930s, it was a gigantic acoustic guitar that stood over five feet tall (not including the 10" endpin) and was played vertically. It had a flat fingerboard, like a guitar's, but the 42" scale length of an upright acoustic bass. The frets were filed flush with the fingerboard, making the Bassoguitar what would now be called a lined fret-

less. It didn't have much of an impact on the music scene, although one was played (and endorsed) by Israel Crosby in the Fletcher Henderson Orchestra.

The Dobro company offered a similar instrument that was an oversize version of its metal-resonator guitars. Like the Regal, it was so big it had to be played standing up. (And wouldn't you just love to hear what *that* sounded like?)

In the late 1930s, Gibson took the idea a step further with its Electric Bass Guitar. (The name was certainly prophetic.) Like the Regal Bassoguitar, this instrument was a huge hollow-body guitar equipped with an endpin for vertical playing. But, unlike the Regal, the Gibson had a magnetic

The Dobro company offered a fretted bass version of their famous resonator guitar. This 1931 promo photo shows one that belonged to the Rancho Revelers. Why they were hanging out next to the airplane is unclear.

Just before World War II, Gibson built two of these beautiful instruments, know simply as Electric Bass Guitars. Nearly five feet tall, they were played vertically (notice the endpin). One of them was used by Wally Kamin in the Les Paul Trio.

pickup (although the only amplifiers available at the time were designed for guitars). According to vintage-guitar authority George Gruhn, two of these unique upright bass guitars were made between 1938 and 1940. One of them ended up in the hands of Wally Kamin, Les Paul's brother-in-law, who used it to accompany the pioneering electric guitarist in his trio. The other was played by the teenage female bassist in a Hawaiian-music group called the Tropical Islanders.

Electric Sticks

While some builders were creating oversize instruments to get better bass sounds, Gibson engineer Lloyd Loar had a different idea: build a *small* instrument and use electricity to make the notes louder. In 1924, Loar reportedly built a prototype of a "stick" bass that was, in concept at least, quite similar to the upright electric basses of today. The pickup was an electrostatic transducer mounted in a Bakelite box under the bridge (and we can only wonder what Loar might have used for an amp). When Gibson was less than enthusiastic about the idea, Loar formed his own company, Vivi-Tone, to market the bass and his other electric instruments. There is no evidence that Vivi-Tone electric basses ever made it into production, although one of Loar's

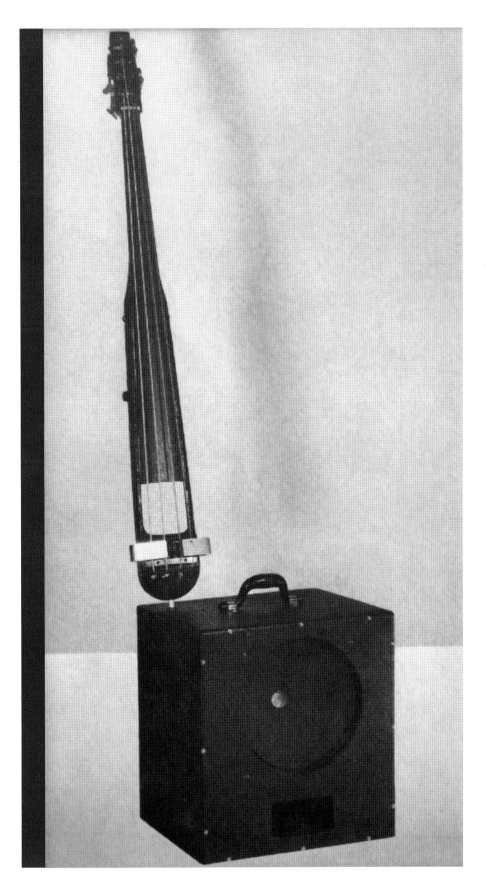

Introduced in 1936, the Rickenbacker Electro Bass-Viol had a metal body and horseshoe-magnet pickup. It could be attached to the top of its amp, and the endpin-to-amp connection also included the output jack. Only a handful of these instruments were made before production ended in 1940.

ELECTRIFIED DOUBLE BASS!
NEW – STARTLING – LONG-NEEDED!

Here is the answer to the Bass player's dream. It is light—It is quickly portable—Full size bass scale; may be bowed, plucked or slapped. Special speaker reproduces true bass tone. It is novel — It is unique — It is very practical. Be the first to show this startling new instrument in your locality.

Specially designed electric pick-up with volume control. Special amplifier to be used only with this instrument.

Every bass player a potential buyer. Fine for all fretted groups as well as orchestras. Operates on 110 volt 60 cycle alternating current.

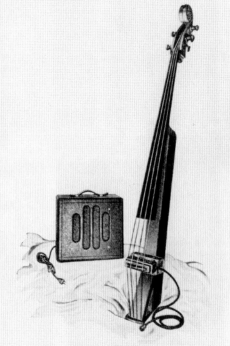

Complete outfit consisting of instrument, carrying case for instrument and amplifier Complete **$180.00**

[25]

The Regal company of Chicago also offered an electric upright in 1936. Like the Rickenbacker Electro Bass-Viol, it came with a companion amp.

apprentices, Bruno Joseph, later built several electric uprights under his own name.

During the 1930s, upright electric basses were offered by several musical instrument companies, including Regal (who seemed to be determined to do *something* different in the bass market). The best known was probably the Rickenbacker Electro Bass-Viol, designed by George Beauchamp. Introduced in 1936, it was a metal "stick" that plugged directly into the top of its amp. Equipped with the familiar Rickenbacker horseshoe-magnet pickup, the Electro Bass-Viol had gut strings that were wrapped with metal foil where they passed through the pickup. In the late 1930s, Columbia released a recording by Mark Allen & His Orchestra,

Zoom, ZOOM, ZOOM,

Zoom, ZOOM, ZOOM,

*Listen to the music of
the Big Bass Viol*

And while you're listening, just imagine standing close to this majestic instrument, your fingers slapping the strings, bringing forth deep, resonant tones—WHAT A THRILL!!!

No. 240KAY

The majestic beauty of this Bass stands unrivalled by the most expensive imports. The top is of spruce and the back of grained curly maple carefully selected and fully swelled. It has a maple neck and ebonized fingerboard and trimmings. It is extremely durable, fully guaranteed and highly recommended for orchestra or school work, where quality, durability, and price are the prime considerations. This instrument can be bowed as well as picked and slapped.

An Oahu Course of Bass Lessons has been written for the new student. Write for information to Dept. C-25 of the Oahu Publishing Company, Cleveland, Ohio.

No. 240KAY—Orchestra Model Bass Viol $120.00
No. 261K—Leather Carrying Strap.. 3.25
No. 241K—Bass Viol Canvas Weatherproof Bag (equipped with pockets for bow and strings) 10.75
No. 321K—Bass Viol Stand. Made of brass and steel, heavily nickel-plated. Adjustable to pitch and angle, permitting Bass to be held on stand in correct position. Folds compactly 15.00

VEGA ELECTRIC BASS VIOL AND AMPLIFIER

Modern science together with modern streamlining has created a new, slim Bass. An easily portable instrument whose smooth, full tones can be made to rise and fall at the player's command.

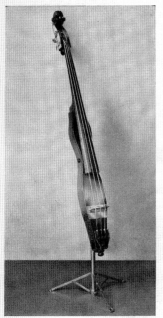

Its wood body is only 6 inches wide; Neck and fingerboard are regulation size; Full plate machine heads; Volume and Tone controls conveniently located on side of body. Body is attached to a plate which slips into a bracket on a heavily-nickel-plated floor stand and is then adjustable for height and tilt. Only a second is required to attach or remove the instrument from its stand; Included is a weatherproof bag with pockets for stand and bow; Gut, metal wound or, in fact, any type of strings may be used.

The 18-watt amplifier used with this Bass is supplied with special rubber mounting to handle the heavy bass vibrations and is recommended for perfect response and clarity of tone.

No. 133K—Complete outfit for 110 volt, 50-60 cycle A.C. operation ..$232.00

Complete outfit for A.C.-D.C. operation 265.00

Bass Viol only, with bag, cord and stand 155.00

13

The Vega electric upright from the 1930s had a curved body and a vibration-sensing pickup. It came with an amp that offered 18 watts of power for "heavy bass vibrations."

featuring the Rickenbacker bass. It may not have been a hit, but it was probably the first record ever made with an electric bass.

The Tutmarc Bass

By the time the United States entered World War II in 1941—which effectively halted all musical instrument research and development—there were gigantic bass guitars and upright electric basses, all of them played vertically. But the idea of a horizontally played electric bass guitar had to wait for Leo Fender...or did it?

In the early 1930s, a steel guitarist named Paul H. Tutmarc built a solid-body electric upright with a magnetic pickup. This cello-sized instrument was never actually produced by Tutmarc's Seattle-based company, Audiovox Manufacturing, but it was an important stepping stone to an even more radical instrument. Years later, Paul's son, Bud Tutmarc, told Mikael Jansson that his father's compassion for bass players spurred the idea: "My dad, being a bandleader and a traveling musician, always felt sorry for the string bass player. The instrument was so large that once the bassist put it in his car, there was only enough room left for him to drive. The other band members would travel together and have much enjoyment, while the bass player was always alone. That is the actual idea that inspired my father to make an electric bass."

In 1935, Paul Tutmarc had another bright idea, one that would free up even more space in the bass player's car. Why not build a really small electric bass that could be played horizontally like a guitar? This idea became the Audiovox Model 736 Electronic Bass, which was a truly startling innovation: a solid-body, fretted 4-string equipped with a magnetic pickup. The scale length was 30½" (close to the short-scale standard that Gibson and other bass manufacturers later favored), and the instrument had a mirror-steel pickguard and a metal bridge. Tutmarc built his steel

In the early 1930s, a steel guitarist named Paul H. Tutmarc built a solid-body electric upright with a magnetic pickup. This cello-sized instrument was never actually produced by Tutmarc's Seattle-based company, Audiovox Manufacturing, but it was an important stepping stone to an even more radical instrument.

The Audiovox Model 736 Electronic Bass and its inventor, Paul Tutmarc of Seattle. Introduced in 1936, the Model 736 was the first solid-body electric bass guitar designed to be played in a horizontal position. Unfortunately, it was ahead of its time and had no commercial or musical impact.

guitars from black walnut, and he used the same wood for the bass. List price was $65.

About 100 Audiovox Model 736 basses were made, and their distribution was apparently limited to the Seattle area. In 1947, Bud Tutmarc revived the idea with a similar instrument he called the Serenader Electric String Bass, but that didn't catch on either. (One of Bud's innovations was the unusual choice of purpleheart wood for the fingerboard. This exotic hardwood has only recently come into common use in guitarmaking. The Tutmarcs were ahead of the curve in many ways!)

The big question is, of course: Did Leo Fender know about the Tutmarc basses? A 1999 article by John Teagle in *Vintage Guitar* magazine speculated that Leo may have at least seen some of the Audiovox ads. Richard R. Smith, the author of *Fender: The Sound Heard 'round the World*—

the definitive work on Leo Fender—doesn't think so. Smith, who interviewed Leo extensively over a period of years, said: "He never told me about it, although Leo and [Fender co-worker] Don Randall were aware of the Rickenbacker Electro standup and the Gibson Mando Bass. This whole case is probably just parallel evolution, like bats and birds. They both have wings but completely different origins."

There's certainly not much resemblance between the Audiovox Model 736 and the original Fender Precision Bass, and the different specifications—especially the scale lengths—tend to support Smith's "parallel evolution" explanation. But we must give Paul Tutmarc credit for conceiving a horizontally played electric bass guitar and building what now appears to be the first functional version (barring any further discoveries of primeval instruments).

It should also be noted that James Thompson, the father of well-known bass builder Carl Thompson, made a one-of-a-kind electric bass guitar in 1942. James Thompson modified a broken Kay archtop guitar by attaching a long neck and crude pickup, and he used this "Frankenstein bass" on his home recordings. On these tapes, the instrument sounds much more like an electric bass guitar than an upright bass.

Clearly, the idea of a fretted electric bass that could be played horizontally like a guitar was a good one. Somebody just had to build one that worked well and that musicians would accept.

Chapter 3: A Bass Is Born

If Leo Fender wanted to "free the bass player from the big doghouse," he also had another constituency in mind. Richard R. Smith told the story in *Fender: The Sound Heard 'round the World*: "As dance bands downsized in the late 1940s, some [guitar] players lost work because they could not double on stand-up bass. According to Leo, they came complaining to him because they did not want to take the time to learn upright techique. They needed a bass they could play like a guitar—a fretted bass."

Leo Fender was not a musician himself, but he always listened closely to the musicians who were his customers and friends. After hearing the guitarists' problem, he began to ponder a solution. Leo had already built and marketed the Broadcaster guitar, later known as the Telecaster. Following the "bigger for bass" approach of the Gibson mando-bass (which he knew about), all he had to do was take his solid-body electric guitar and make it bigger. And so he did.

The original Fender Precision Bass was very much like a big Telecaster. It had a square-sided ash body and a bolt-on maple neck. Figuring out how long to make the neck was one of the more challenging engineering

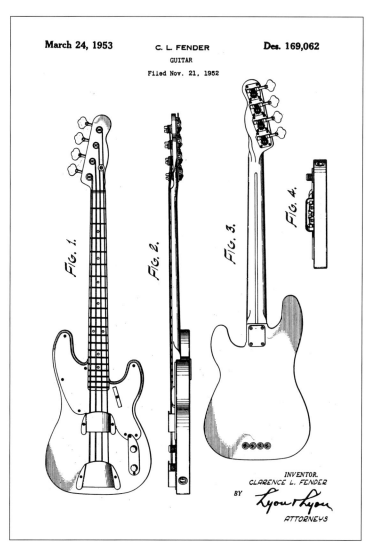

March 24, 1953   C. L. FENDER   Des. 169,062
GUITAR
Filed Nov. 21, 1952

FIG. 1.   FIG. 2.   FIG. 3.   FIG. 4.

INVENTOR.
CLARENCE L. FENDER
BY Lyon + Lyon
ATTORNEYS

The design patent for the Fender Precision Bass was not filed until almost a year after the instrument was introduced. Apparently, Leo Fender was not too concerned anyone would try to steal his idea.

Based on the Telecaster guitar, the Fender Precision Bass had an ash body and a bolt-on maple neck. The chrome covers concealed a single-coil pickup and a two-saddle bridge equipped with a string mute.

problems. According to Smith, Leo Fender used information in a physics textbook that belonged to secretary Elizabeth Nagel Hayzlett, a UCLA student, to come up with a 34" scale length. But George Fullerton, who worked with Leo for many years, said it was more a matter of trial and error: "We tried some shorter scales like 30" and 32", but they didn't seem to get the resonance we needed. We may have even tried something like a 36" scale, but when we got to that length the distance between the frets was too wide to be practical for a player."

However they did it, 34" was an uncannily accurate choice. It has proven to be the standard for 4-strings ever since. It also fit nicely between the 25 1/2" scale of the Telecaster guitar and the 40–42" scale lengths of most upright basses.

Leo chose the name "Precision Bass" largely because the instrument was fretted and therefore had more precise intonation than an upright with its fretless fingerboard. Smith says the name also refers to the "precise" (focused) tone of the instrument and the accuracy of the Fender factory's machines, which were more precise than traditional guitar builders' hand tools.

The prototype had tuning machines adapted from an upright and steel-wrapped gut strings. (For the production instruments, Fender ordered flatwound steel strings from the V.C. Squier company.) Because the body was so large, Leo gave it cutaways for better balance, creating a shape that foreshadowed his 1953 design for the Stratocaster guitar. The pickup was a simple single-coil design, with one polepiece directly below each string. There were two knurled control knobs: volume and tone. Anticipating that musicians would pluck the strings with their thumb, Leo included a finger rest mounted below the strings on the large black-plastic pickguard. The bridge had two saddles made of pressed fiber. Chrome covers concealed both the pickup and the bridge. These were not merely decorative: the pickup cover provided electronic shielding, and the bridge cover contained a rubber string mute.

It's easy for contemporary bass players, accustomed to the sustain of high-fidelity instruments with roundwound strings, to forget that the Precision Bass was intended to mimic the sound of an upright. Leo Fender knew that if his odd new instrument were going to be accepted, it would have to serve the same function as "the big doghouse." Even though the flatwound strings sounded incredibly dead by modern standards, they still sustained longer than the gut strings players used on uprights. That's why Leo included a mute to deaden the sound and produce short, thumping notes.

The second part of the equation was the amplifier. Leo Fender knew that the Rickenbacker upright electric bass had been sold with a companion amp, and he quickly determined that his standard guitar amps could not handle the low frequencies his new bass generated. So he set to work creating a new amp, which became the first Fender Bassman. "Especially designed for bass reproduction," the Bassman had a single Jensen 15" speaker and a 26-watt tube amp with enough power to produce a reasonable bass sound at low to medium volumes.

Not many people have heard what the original Precision Bass sounded like when it was introduced, but one person who has is guitar and bass designer Rich Lasner. "I took an original P-Bass, with flatwound strings as it would have been delivered and set up to the specs that they used, with the mute in the cover," he told me. "I played it through an original Bassman amp at medium volume and listened to what it was supposed to sound like. It's the loudest upright bass you ever heard."

Surging Undertow

Fender introduced the Precision Bass late in 1951, to little fanfare. Many in the music industry loooked upon Leo's solid-body electric guitars with skepticism, and they saw his strange bass contraption as further proof he was crazy.

The first real sign of acceptance came in an unexpected area: jazz. Leo Fender had thought his bass would be looked upon favorably by guitarists in country-western music (his favorite style), but few country musicians showed any interest in it. One exception was Joel Price, who reportedly bought the first Precision Bass sent to Nashville and played it at the Grand Ole Opry in 1952. While Leo may have noted that event with some satisfaction, it's safe to assume he didn't think one of his new basses would be publicized for its use in a well-known jazz group. But life is full of surprises.

After he introduced the Precision Bass, Leo Fender actively promoted its use, often going to concerts and nightclubs to show it to musicians. Sometime in early 1952 he was in New York City, where he encountered jazz vibraphonist and bandleader Lionel Hampton. Many years later, Hampton related the tale to bassist Christian Fabian. According to Fabian: "Lionel told me that he was at a jam session with his bassist, Roy Johnson, where they met 'the guy who invented that thing,' meaning Leo Fender. Roy went up on the bandstand and tried it. Lionel said that people booed him, because he was a jazz bassist playing this electric bass. But Lionel really liked the sound, and Leo Fender told him he could keep the bass. Right after that, they took it on a tour of the South. Lionel said that everywhere they played, it got a lot of attention. People would come up afterwards and ask about it. Leo Fender had given Lionel his phone number, and he gave it to the people who were asking about the bass. He said that after a month, Fender must have had 100 orders for the bass."

In the July 30, 1952, issue of *Down Beat*, Leonard Feather reported on an unusual occurrence at a Lionel Hampton gig: "Suddenly we observed that there was something wrong with the band. It didn't have a bass player. And yet—we heard a bass. On a second glance we noticed something even odder. There were two guitars—but we

Hamp shows off the new bass to Billy May and the Johnnie Rays.

New Instruments

Hamp-lified Fiddle May Lighten Bassists' Burdens

By LEONARD FEATHER

New York—Do you happen to be a bass player, or sympathize with anyone who is?

Have you ever lugged your instrument from the bus, up five flights of stairs, or across a crowded street on a hot summer day?

Have you ever had to submit to those corny gags about the near-sighted landlady who says you can't take that girl to your room?

Well, maybe your worrying days will soon be over.

A bass-ic revolution has been going on quietly in music circles. It first became apparent some months ago when Lionel Hampton's band played a gig in town. Suddenly we observed that there was something wrong with the band. It didn't have a bass player. And yet—we heard a bass. On a second glance we noticed something even odder. There were two guitars—but we only heard one. And then the picture became clearer. Sitting next to the guitarist was someone who held what looked like a guitar at first glance, but on closer inspection revealed a long, fretted neck and a peculiarly shaped body, with electric controls and a wire running to a speaker.

"Sure, man," said Hamp excitedly when we asked him later, "that's our electric bass. We've had it for months!"

He introduced us to Roy Johnson, the Kansas City bassist who for all these months had been trudging around the country, unheralded, playing this sensational instrumental innovation.

Easy Going

"It's no trouble at all," he declared. "I learned to play it right away; in fact I used it on the job the same day I got it. Tunes the same as a regular bass."

"But," said Lionel, "it sounds two octaves deeper!"

And on the next set, listening more carefully, we listened and were duly impressed by the deep, booming quality, the ability

up a little above normal, cut through the whole bottom of the band like a surging undertow.

It wasn't the first time an electric bass had been heard, of course. Many years ago, in the 1930s, Mose Allen in the old Jimmie Lunceford band started toting around what looked like a bodiless bass, a skeleton instrument, but the regulation length. At that time bass amplification had not attained its present degree of finesse, and the results were little, if any, better than those produced by the traditional wooden bass violin. Chubby Jackson and others have added an amp to the regular bass (or to Chubby's five-stringed innovation).

Wee Whale

But Roy Johnson has himself a whale of a plaything—a whale built like a sprat, to boot. He and Lionel have the only two models available at this writing, but the inventor, a Los Angeleno, expects to put them on the market soon.

"Not only that," says Lionel, "but we're going to have him make some supersonic vibes that'll work like an accordion, so you can make chords without striking all the notes. It'll have softer mallets because there'll be all kinds of tone control. Wait'll you see it!"

We're on tenterhooks. And any day now, we expect to see a blueprint for an 88-key, supersonic portable piano.

Date With Dickenson

New York—Vic Dickenson, veteran trombonist now at Lou Terrasi's in New York, returned to wax

The Fender Precision Bass got a boost from publicity in the July 30, 1952, issue of *Down Beat*. In an article entitled "Hamp-lified Fiddle May Lighten Bassists' Burdens," noted jazz critic Leonard Feather praised the new instrument for its "deep, booming quality."

only heard one. And then the picture became clearer. Sitting next to the guitarist was someone who was holding what looked like a guitar at first glance, but on closer inspection revealed a long, fretted neck and a peculiarly shaped body, with electric controls and a wire running to a speaker."

What *Down Beat* called a "Hamp-lified fiddle" was a Fender Precision Bass. Lionel Hampton had gotten one of the first production models and decided it was just the thing he needed to draw attention to his band. Roy Johnson told Feather that he had had no trouble adjusting to the new instrument because it "tunes the same as a regular bass."

Feather went on to praise the Precision's "deep, booming quality," noting that "the bass, its volume turned up a little above normal, cut through the whole bottom of the band like a surging undertow." Those words would prove prophetic. That ability to "cut through" and provide "surging" power to the bottom end would eventually start a revolution in music that would resonate outward into all of popular culture.

Later in 1952, Monk Montgomery replaced Roy Johnson as Hampton's bassist. The brother of well-known jazz guitarist Wes Montgomery, Monk had been strictly an upright bass player—until then. "Hamp handed me the Fender and told me he wanted

Fender offered the Precision Bass with a matching Bassman amplifier. The combination produced a bass sound that was close to that of an upright—but louder.

FRETTED NECK
SUPERB TONE
EASILY PLAYED
MODERN DESIGN
HIGHLY PORTABLE
EXTREMELY RUGGED
FASTER CHANGES
A NEW PLAYING
SENSATION

LIGHT WEIGHT
1/6 SIZE REGULAR BASS
NOW IN USE BY
MANY OF AMERICA'S
LEADING ARTISTS

BASSMAN AMPLIFIER
• Especially designed for bass reproduction
• Custom designed Jensen; 15" Jensen speaker
• True fidelity bass reproduction
• Excellent volume characteristic
• Rugged construction

DISTRIBUTED EXCLUSIVELY BY

RADIO & TELEVISION EQUIPMENT CO.

207 OAK STREET   SANTA ANA, CALIF.

Monk Montgomery's playing in the Lionel Hampton band helped to publicize the Fender Precision Bass in the early 1950s.

this electric instrument sound in the band," Monk later told Mike Newman of *Guitar Player*. "The electric bass was considered a bastard instrument. Conventional bass players despised it. It was new and a threat to what they knew…. At first I freaked out, because I was in love with my upright bass…[but] I made up my mind to do it and did it well."

The new Fender basses turned up in a few other places. Early Fender ads featured Shifte Henry, a New York bassist who played with jazz and jump bands, praising his new P-Bass as "the most." But Leo Fender's quest to free bassists from the doghouse wasn't going to be easy. Most of them were not about to adopt this "bastard instrument" (an attitude that pre-

New York bassist Shifte Henry was an early endorser of the Fender Precision Bass. (He also turned up in the lyrics of the Elvis Presley hit "Jailhouse Rock.")

vails, to some extent, in jazz to this day). And the guitarists Leo was trying to help didn't jump at the chance to play the new instrument, either. But that didn't matter. The Precision Bass would soon assume a prominent role in another style of music that would push it into the foreground—a brand-new kind of music called rock & roll.

Chapter 4: Butterflies & Basses

In *Chaos: Making a New Science*, James Gleick wrote: "The modern study of chaos began with the creeping realization…that quite simple mathematical equations could model systems every bit as violent as a waterfall. Tiny differences in input could quickly become overwhelming differences in output—a phenomenon given the name 'sensitive dependence on initial conditions.' In weather, for example, this translates into what is only half-jokingly known as the Butterfly Effect—the notion that a butterfly stirring the air today in Peking can transform storm systems next month in New York."

Or, perhaps, a Fender Precision Bass stirring the low end in the 1950s could be the "butterfly" in a musical system that would deeply affect many Americans (especially young ones) and contribute to profound changes in culture and society. To understand how this may have occurred, it's necessary to reconsider a widely accepted notion: that the invention of the electric guitar led directly to the rock & roll era.

For one thing, electric guitars had been around since the 1930s. The Rickenbacker "frying pan," generally considered to be the first electric guitar, was introduced in 1932. Spanish-style guitars with magnetic pickups followed within a few years, and Les Paul created his famous "Log" (an early solid-body electric guitar) in 1941. By

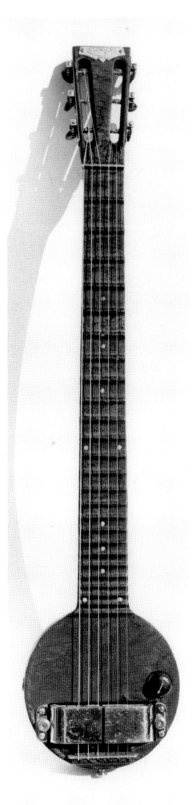

Introduced in 1932, Rickenbacker's A-25 "frying pan" guitar was the first production electric guitar equipped with a magnetic pickup. It was a lap steel; Spanish-style electric guitars followed a few years later.

1951, the electric guitar and the guitar amp had benefited from numerous technological improvements for nearly 20 years, but rock & roll was just beginning to stir. The modern drum kit—the other key ingredient of a rock band—had also been around since the 1930s.

The prototypical rock & roll bands usually featured one or two electric guitars, a drum set, and an upright bass. (Keyboards were unusual,

except in the case of Jerry Lee Lewis—who tended to treat his piano as a percussion instrument.) The "doghouse" bass could lay down a rudimentary foundation, but it suffered as the music got louder, often sounding more like lower-register percussion than a pitched instrument (especially played in the slap style employed by bassists such as Bill Black, who backed Elvis Presley). As Elvis showed, you could get pretty "gone" with this instrumentation, but there was still a need for an instrument that could assert a well-defined bass sound and enable the music to get louder (and therefore more powerful). Some of the small groups of the early

The modern drum kit developed after World War I and was a key element of the sound of the big bands of the 1930s. By the mid '30s, both the electric guitar and the drum kit were available to musicians, but the birth of rock & roll was still almost 20 years away.

In early 1955, the polepieces of the Precision pickup were set to staggered heights to balance the volume between the strings. Leo Fender continued to tinker with his design, hoping that by improving its sound and playability it would receive more widespread acceptance among musicians.

1950s hinted at this, and it's no coincidence that Samuel "Jay" Guy played a Precision Bass in Louis Jordan's popular jump band. It made a big difference in the impact of the music.

The power of a strong, loud bass instrument seems remarkably obvious (at least to bass players), but most of the histories of popular music focus on the electric guitar as the crucial instrument in the evolution of rock & roll. It played an absolutely essential role, to be sure—but it was really the Fender bass that made possible the forward progress of this new genre. Without it, rock & roll might never have moved beyond the crude (if captivating) sound of the young Elvis on "That's All Right" or Chuck Berry on "Maybellene."

The Fender bass arrived at a crucial turning point in the saga of American popular music. In 1951, tastes were changing: the big bands were dying out and small groups were ascendant. Jump tunes—which would prove to be a bridge to rock & roll—were becoming more and more popular, and the climate was right for a strong new sound in the rhythm section.

If we pull back and look at the wider picture, we see that the American public was enjoying the domestic calm (and renewed production of consumer goods) of the post-World War II era, but international relations were tense. The United States was engaged in a nerve-racking Cold War with the Soviet Union and Communist China. Schoolchildren held drills in which they "prepared" for nuclear attack by kneeling in the hallway and covering their heads with their hands. In 1952, army general Dwight D. Eisenhower was elected president, and his secretary of state, John Foster Dulles, soon announced a U.S. policy of massive retaliation in response to any Soviet threat. The specter of annihilation always loomed in the background.

Despite this tension, popular culture in America had reached new heights (or depths) of blandness and conformity. Art was a Norman Rockwell painting on the cover of the *Saturday Evening Post*, and the cinema was dominated by overblown Hollywood epics like *The Ten Commandments*. Fashion was defined by the man in the gray flannel suit (and his wife in her housedress). Television was showing some promise as a new popular artform, but it would soon be condemned as a "vast wasteland." In music, the Pop charts assembled by *Billboard* magazine—which reflected mainstream listening tastes—were filled with lightweight tunes cranked out by an army of faceless studio musicians. In the recording studios, the upright bass still reigned supreme—but that was about to change.

In 1954, Leo Fender altered the design of the
Precision Bass and gave it the contoured body style
featured on the newly introduced Stratocaster guitar.
The standard finish was a two-color sunburst, comple-
mented by a white-plastic pickguard. The Bassman
amp was also upgraded to a 4x10 configuration that
became legendary—as a guitar amp.

Chapter 5: Jail Break

There has been a great deal of debate about what was the first rock & roll song, but one thing is clear: the bass players on all of the early rock & roll recordings were using uprights. Whether it was Bill Haley on "Rock Around the Clock" or Elvis Presley belting out "Heartbreak Hotel," they were backed by guys slapping away furiously on doghouses.

The Fender Precision Bass made modest inroads after its introduction, but it remained something of a curiosity in the mid '50s. There are photos and accounts of players using P-Basses in a few country and rhythm

In 1957, Leo Fender once again redesigned the Precision Bass. The new version featured a redesigned headstock and a gold-anodized aluminum pickguard. This proved to be the "final" version of the instrument, which has changed little since then.

One of the most important changes on the '57 Precision Bass was a new pickup that had a double-coil humbucking design. (A humbucking pickup cancels electromagnetic noise by using two coils wired out of phase and two magnets oriented with opposite polarities. The result is quieter sound.) The new pickup featured two polepieces for each string, a design Leo Fender believed offered a less harsh attack transient and would save speakers.

& blues bands, and a film clip of a Fender bassist backing a young Jerry Lee Lewis on "Great Balls of Fire" appears in the documentary *The Golden Age of Rock & Roll*. But Jerry Lee was the exception, even among rockers.

Elvis Presley apparently recognized the potential of the new instrument, and he worked hard trying to convince his bassist, Bill Black, to use a Fender bass. In *Last Train to Memphis: The Rise of Elvis Presley*, Peter Guralnick described the 1957 recording of the *Jailhouse Rock* movie soundtrack: "Bill Black was feeling increasingly frustrated not just at the indifference with which he saw himself and [guitarist] Scotty [Moore] being treated but by his own difficulties in trying to learn how to play the electric bass. . . . Bill had only recently gotten a Fender bass of his own, and he couldn't get the ominous, rhythmic intro to Leiber and Stoller's 'You're So Square (Baby, I Don't Care),' one of the highlights of the film score. He tried it again and again, got more and more pissed off and embarrassed by his failure, and finally just slammed the bass down, slid it across the floor, and stormed out of the studio, while everyone watched in disbelief."

Although he had some problems switching from upright, Bill Black brought the sound of the Fender Precision Bass to millions of listeners on Elvis Presley's "Jailhouse Rock," a big hit in 1957.

Guralnick goes on to report that Presley himself picked up the Precision and played the song's bass line—including the intro, with its "ominous" repeated hammer-on. This tune is worth a listen, because it's one of the earliest rock & roll songs where the sound of a Fender bass plays a featured role. And the fact Elvis himself played the part makes it that much more intriguing. (It's available on various collections, including the monumental RCA box set *Elvis: The King of Rock 'n' Roll: The Complete 50's Masters*.)

Bill Black eventually became more comfortable with his Fender bass, which is important because it brought the sound of this still-new instrument to the ears of millions of Elvis fans. (Most of whom, admittedly, were not focusing on the bass player.) "Jailhouse Rock," with Black on P-Bass, was the No. 3 Pop song of 1957, and it probably deserves credit as the first major hit featuring an electric bass. This breakthrough was reinforced by the movie, where Black was seen playing—or at least holding—his Fender bass in the famous dance scene that has been called the first music video.

Bill Black has received little credit for his role as one of the pioneers of the electric bass, but it's worth noting that his post-Elvis group, the Bill Black Combo, had a 1959 instrumental hit called "Smokie, Part 2." (It's on *Hi Times: The Hi Records R&B Years*, a three-CD anthology on Right Stuff/Capitol.) The tune went to No. 1 on the R&B charts and No. 17 on the Pop charts—and it featured the unmistakable punch of a Precision Bass.

Rhythm & Bass

In rhythm & blues, the sound of the Fender bass was accepted somewhat more readily than it was in mainstream pop. In his book *The Death of Rhythm & Blues*, Nelson George provided a thoughtful analysis of the impact of the Fender bass on '50s R&B: "The electric bass forever altered the relationship between the rhythm section, the horns, and the other melodic instruments. To Quincy Jones, who at the time was splitting his arranging skills between big band, jazz, and pop, 'It really changed the sound of music because it ate up so much space. Its sound was imposing in comparison to the upright bass, so it couldn't have the same function. You couldn't just have it playing 4/4 lines because it had too much personality. Before the electric bass and the electric guitar, the rhythm section was the support section, backing up the horns and the piano. But when they were introduced, everything upstairs had to take a back seat. The rhythm section became the stars. All because of this technological development. The old style didn't work anymore and it created a new language.'"

Guitarist Dave Myers picked up a Precision Bass in 1958 and changed the sound of Chicago blues. Within a few years, large horn bands had been replaced by small, highly amplified groups in most of the city's nightclubs.

George went on to say: "The electric bass had a punchy, dynamic range that would become identified with rhythm & blues. Moreover R&B musicians' willingness to integrate new technology into their vision would make their sound, despite its many detractors, as consistently innovative as any genre of American music in the coming years. The [bass] patterns of [songwriter Jesse] Stone and others, in conjunction with the increased use of the electric bass in the '50s, would turn this country's ears around."

One of the musicians who accepted the "new technology" of the Fender bass—after some initial reluctance—was the Chicago blues guitarist Dave Myers. Since the early 1950s, Dave had teamed with his brother Louis in a popular group called the Four Aces. Louis played lead guitar while Dave backed him using a style that combined chords with bass lines played low on the *E* string. In 1958, Dave Myers encountered a Precision Bass on a visit to a music store, where "this fellow named Harry" encouraged him to give it a try. "I looked at that thing in that freak case," Myers told Bill Milkowski, "and it looked like some antique in a coffin or something! I asked Harry what it was. 'A bass? There's a bass over there.' I was pointing to an upright in the back. He said, 'No, no, no—this is the same. It's just something you have to get used to.' I said I didn't think I could ever play it. The strings were too big."

Harry eventually convinced Myers to take the P-Bass home with him. His first attempt at playing it wasn't successful—he immediately blew the speakers in his guitar amp. He borrowed another amp and tried again, with the same result. "Finally, the Fender peoples came out to my house to check the bass," recalled Myers. "They asked me what did I think of it. I told 'em it had done blown up two amplifiers for me, so they came back about a month later with an amplifier called a Bassman. That's when I really got a load of this thing. I hooked that amp up, and boy, did the sound come out beautiful. Man, when I heard that I knew good and well. The sound was so deep and beautiful, it was amazing. And it was twice as loud as an acoustic."

Myers immediately began to play his Precision Bass on gigs in Chicago and throughout the Midwest. It electrified audiences. ("They would be standing up on their chairs and going wild. That's when I knew I really had something going with that Fender bass.") With Dave Myers leading the way, the Chicago blues groups began to adopt Fender basses,

and small ensembles that featured amplified instruments soon dominated the scene. "Word got around in Chicago," said Myers, "and the
club owners in the big joints began saying, 'What's the use of hiring 18
or 25 pieces when four pieces can do the job?' And they dropped the big
band like a hot potato. That damn Fender Precision Bass knocked them
out of the pocket."

It was a sign of things to come. But this was well before the civil rights
movement, and the divide between black and white music remained deep
and wide. Young African-Americans might drop into a nightclub to see a
blues band with a Fender bassist or dig the "imposing" sound of a P-Bass
on an R&B record, but white teenagers were still hearing mostly acoustic
bass on the pop tunes that dominated the mainstream airwaves. "Jailhouse Rock" had made its mark, though—and the tide was turning.

Chapter 6: Ride the Wild Bass

Soon after Elvis Presley's "Jailhouse Rock" hit the charts, another important electric-bass advance occurred during the sessions for Duane Eddy's "Rebel Rouser." An instrumental hit in 1958, this memorable rocker features two bassists; as Tony Bacon explained in *The Bass Book*: "Jimmy Simmons plays double bass to give depth and tone to the bass line, while Buddy Wheeler plays the same notes on electric bass guitar, adding a percussive, attacking edge." Duane Eddy has confirmed that Wheeler was playing a Fender bass; this song is probably the first example of the two-bass system later used on many recordings in Nashville, where it acquired the name "tic-tac" bass.

Although "Rebel Rouser" had a standard Fender 4-string doubling the upright part, another electric bass became the preferred axe for tic-tac: the Danelectro UB2 6-string (tuned like a guitar, *EADGBE*, but down an octave). Introduced in 1956, the UB2 was essentially a solid-body guitar with an extra-long, two-octave neck. (The scale length was 29^1/$_2$"—well short of Fender's 34").

For the tic-tac sound, the percussive attack of the Dano 6-string was used to double the thump of an upright, creating a bass part that was both deep and well defined. While heard occasionally on rock & roll songs, it became a staple of country sessions. (As David Hungate noted in *Bass Player*, the tic-tac Dano, usually played by Harold Bradley, was "an integral part of most Nashville rhythm sections throughout most of the [late] '50s and '60s.")

In addition to Danelectro, several other companies brought electric basses on the market in the mid to late '50s. These included Kay, which offered a bargain-basement model for folks who found the original Preci-

(L) Nathan Daniel of Danelectro came up with a different kind of bass guitar in 1956: a 6-string instrument tuned like a guitar (*EADGBE*) but down an octave. It was used on some early rock & roll records, but its most important role was in the "tic-tac" two-bass system heard on many Nashville recordings of the late '50s and '60s. This distinctive Long Horn version of the bass was introduced in 1958.

(R) One of the most important early competitors to the Fender bass was the Rickenbacker Model 4000. Introduced in 1957, it was the first electric bass to employ neck-through-body construction, a design innovation that would prove to have lasting impact.

sion Bass a bit too pricey at $199.50, and Gibson, with their violin-bodied Electric Bass. The most innovative competitor was Rickenbacker, whose first electric bass, the Model 4000, showed up in music stores in 1957.

Roger's Idea

What set the Rickenbacker Model 4000 apart, even more than its distinctive body shape or massive horseshoe pickup, was its construction method: it was the first neck-through-body bass.

Before the Rick 4000, electric basses had been assembled from separate necks and bodies. Fender used the bolt-on approach, while other companies preferred to glue the neck to the body. But when Roger Rossmeisl sat down to design his first electric bass, neither method appealed to him. Rossmeisl was a German luthier who had immigrated to the United States in the early '50s, originally to work for Gibson in Kalamazoo, Michigan. By 1954, he had moved on to the Rickenbacker plant in Southern California, where he soon had primary responsibility for designing the company's electric guitars. Rossmeisl's creations included both hollow-body instruments inspired by the jazz guitars he had learned to build in Germany and solid-bodies that would compete with the new Fender and Gibson models. In 1956, Rickenbacker introduced his Combo 400, a guitar that featured neck-through-body construction.

The idea of building a guitar with a neck that ran the full length of the body did not originate with Rossmeisl. Steel guitars were one-piece instruments, and the Slingerland company offered a "Spanish neck" version of one of its Hawaiian guitars as early as 1939. The best-known pre-1950 example of a neck-through guitar is probably the instrument California luthier Paul Bigsby built for Merle Travis in 1947 or '48. (This was a highly influential guitar, with a body shape that would reappear almost unchanged in the Gibson Les Paul and a peghead design that showed up on the Fender Stratocaster.)

Rossmeisl was proud of his status as a *gitarrenbaumeister* (master guitar builder), and one of the things he liked about neck-through construction was the high degree of craftsmanship it required. With separate necks and bodies, production problems are easy to correct—but the unified structure of a neck-through has less margin for error. Rossmeisl also saw practical advantages. The 1957 Rickenbacker catalog touted the 4000's "full-length neck with two double metal adjusting rods" and noted that "the fact that the tailpiece, bridge, nut, and patent [tuning] heads are mounted on the same piece of wood assures the player of maintaining a straight neck."

Interestingly, there was no mention of sustain, clarity, or other sonic advantages in the early product literature. This isn't too surprising; sustain was not a design goal in an era when the indistinct thump of a gut-string upright was considered the ideal bass tone. And the crude amplifiers of the 1950s were not yet ready for the demands of high-fidelity bass instruments. It would be years before all the advantages of Rossmeisl's design could be fully appreciated.

Surf's Up

The Rickenbacker 4000's innovative design would eventually prove to be influential, but in the late '50s the Fender Precision Bass led the way. In fact, the term "Fender bass" was used generically for years to describe *any* electric 4-string, regardless of manufacturer. And the musicians' union lumped all electric bassists together under the heading "Fender bass."

As the 1950s drew to a close, the low end was getting more and more attention. Quite a few hit songs from that era were based on twangy licks played on Fender or Danelectro basses—or, sometimes, just by whacking the low *E* string of a standard electric guitar. That's what Eddie Cochran did on "Summertime Blues" (1958), which has sometimes been described as a song with electric bass. Not true—but clearly lots of low-end presence didn't hurt.

Surf music was the first style in which a Fender bass was an absolute requirement. And it didn't hurt that Brian Wilson of the Beach Boys usually appeared onstage with a white Precision Bass.

Nokie Edwards gave the punchy sound of the Precision Bass a big boost on the immortal instrumental "Walk—Don't Run," a hit for the Ventures in 1960. (Edwards, originally the group's bassist, later switched to lead guitar.) The tune was highly influential, especially among 1960s California surf bands—many of which were equipped top to bottom with matching Fender instruments.

In a 1997 article in *Vintage Guitar* magazine, Peter Stuart Kohman wrote: "The surf/instrumental rock genres of the early 1960s were crucial proving grounds for the still-newfangled electric bass, and many of the seminal records in these two interrelated styles are also showcases for the Fender bass sound. You can't really imagine surf music without a Fender bass—this is not true of any earlier rock & roll style. During this era, *the bass guitar went from optional to essential equipment* and set up the electric bass for its dominant role in the British Invasion, folk rock, and all that followed [italics mine]."

Kohman goes on to point out that the bassists in budding surf bands played different types of electric basses, including Harmony and Danelectro instruments, but it was a sign of success to have a shiny new Fender bass, usually in a custom color like Candy Apple Red or Lake Placid Blue. The musicians who played these flashy Fenders approached them like guitars rather than uprights, playing downstrokes with a flatpick and going for a tighter, more focused sound than the thud of an acoustic bass. The instrument's potential was just beginning to be tapped.

Fender offered a few custom-color basses as early as 1954. Originally chosen for a practical reason—solid colors masked the flaws in wood unsuitable for blond or sunburst finishes—exotic colors like Foam Green and Shell Pink became very popular, especially with the surf bands of the early 1960s.

A Word from Keef

No less an authority than Keith Richards of the Rolling Stones—a man who knows an awful lot about rhythm—has remarked on the revolutionary impact of the Fender bass in the late 1950s. In a 1989 *Guitar Player* interview, he evaluated the evolution of rock & roll rhythm: "It suddenly changed in '58, '59, '60, until it was all over by the early '60s. The drummers were starting to play eight to the bar, and I thought at first maybe they were just going for more power. Then I realized that, no, it was because of the *bass*, the advent of reliable electric bass guitar. The traditional double bass went bye-bye, this thing that's taller than most guys that play the goddamn thing [*laughs*]. The guitar players were being relegated to bass. If you didn't even have a bass, you could tune down a guitar and play four strings; once you had an actual bass, it was much louder than an acoustic pumping eight to the bar. And the natural inclination of the drummer is then to pick up on what the new bass is doing, because that's what you've got to follow."

Much louder. That was the key. The Fender bass gave bass players a new, assertive identity in rock & roll. They could take a more prominent role in the music and use different bass patterns—and this would have a huge impact on how music was written and performed.

As the "new bass" was gaining its foothold, the U.S. was moving into an era of profound social change. In 1960, John F. Kennedy was elected president, signaling an abrupt end to the conservative complacency of the Eisenhower years. In contrast to his predecessor, Kennedy was young and vigorous, and he launched the space program that would send Americans to the moon by the end of the decade. Jacqueline Kennedy, the First Lady, brought a new sense of style and grace to the White House. The country was infatuated with Jack and Jackie, and few Americans were concerned when their popular president began to increase U.S. involvement in the faraway country of Vietnam. That decision would prove to have dire consequences.

Despite the continuing Cold War, the future seemed brighter with JFK in charge. The *Billboard* Top 40 was still more schlock than rock—the No. 1 song of 1960 was "Theme from 'A Summer Place'" by Percy Faith—but Top 40 tunes by artists such as Elvis Presley ("It's Now or Never"), Roy Orbison ("Only the Lonely"), Jackie Wilson ("Night"), and Duane Eddy ("Because They're Young") indicated a big new sound was making waves.

Chapter 7: Carol & Joe

Carol Kaye, a guitarist, began to play Fender bass in 1963 as a last-minute sub for a bassist who didn't show up for a recording session. Within two years, she was the No. 1 studio bass player in Los Angeles. Her standard setup during the '60s was a Precision Bass with medium-gauge flatwound strings, which she played with a pick. Kaye's solid sound can be heard on dozens of hit records, including the Beach Boys' "Good Vibrations" and Simon & Garfunkel's "Homeward Bound."

In the recording studios of the early 1960s, the dominance of the upright was slipping. The use of tic-tac, with an electric bass doubling the acoustic part, was becoming more common—and sometimes producers wanted *three* basses: an upright, a Fender 4-string, and a Danelectro 6-string. (Recognizing the popularity of the Dano bass, Leo Fender came up with his own version, the Fender Bass VI, in 1961.)

A few producers, though, dared to call for a Fender bass alone—especially if it was being played by studio ace Carol Kaye. She explained why to G. Brown: "I played with a pick, and my sound accidentally put the

Like Carol Kaye, Joe Osborn was a guitarist who picked up the Fender bass as a second instrument—and quickly became a first-call studio bassist. Osborn got an early Jazz Bass in 1960, and he subsequently used the instrument on hundreds of sessions. In 1974, he began to collect signatures on the back of the bass: "The requirement was that I had played on one hit record with that person."

other adjunct bassists out of work—unfortunately. It was more versatile; I could get a deep bass sound or add a bit of 'click' with the pick, enough to make it sound like a Dano at times. That changed the whole thing. The producers started to figure, 'Instead of three bassists, we can hire that one Fender bass player.'"

Kaye was a Los Angeles guitarist who had picked up a Precision Bass in 1963 when the contracted bassist didn't show up for a Capitol Records session. She soon realized that a guitarist who doubled on Fender bass *could* get more work, just as Leo Fender had hoped when he created the Precision Bass.

Kaye is quick to note that the Fender bass had been used on sessions

This 1959 Jazz Bass prototype has a three-knob setup. The first production models featured two "stacked" knobs, but Fender later returned to the three-knob arrangementl.

The '59 Jazz Bass prototype had two unusual pickups: a five-pole pickup in the neck position and a four-pole at the bridge. Leo Fender eventually decided to use two eight-pole pickups, with a pair of polepieces for each string.

for several years before she began to play it. "Since 1955, Ray Pohlman had been doing about 90 percent of the recording on Fender bass in the L.A. studios. He played mostly with his thumb—that's Ray you hear on the Righteous Brothers' 'You've Lost That Lovin' Feelin'"; I played rhythm guitar [on that track]. Ray gave up playing bass to direct the band on the *Shindig* television show. There were a few string bassists who could play Fender bass—Buddy Clarke and Red Callender—but the guitar players usually didn't have the feel of the bass."

Kaye's considerable skill as a sight-reader, combined with the tape-

The Fender Jazz Bass was introduced in 1960. It had a slim neck that was narrower at the nut than the neck of a Precision Bass. The two stacked knobs had a tone control above a volume control. The J-Bass was not actually popular among jazz bassists, at least at first, but many converted guitarists found its easy-playing neck inviting. Leo Fender was probably pleased by that, since he had invented his electric bass with guitarists in mind.

friendly sound she got by playing with a pick, soon made her much in demand as a session bassist. Her early work included pop hits like "Spanish Eyes" by Al Martino and "Whipped Cream" by Herb Alpert & the Tijuana Brass. By 1965, she was the first-call bassist in L.A. Her strong playing was featured on dozens of tracks made by famed producers Phil Spector and Quincy Jones, and her studio log includes the Beach Boys, Ray Charles, Frank Sinatra, Simon & Garfunkel, and a bevy of Motown groups. While she was unknown outside of a small circle of studio players and producers, Kaye was instrumental in bringing the sound of the Fender Precision Bass to the ears of millions of listeners.

In late 1961 and early 1962, Fender began to produce Jazz Basses with three knobs rather than the "stack knob" configuration used on early production models. The two large knobs are separate volume controls for the pickups; the smaller knob is a master tone control that provides passive treble cut.

A year after the Jazz Bass was introduced, Fender offered the Bass VI. Patterned on the Danelectro 6-string bass, the Bass VI was usually tuned like a guitar but an octave lower. (A baritone tuning was sometimes used.) It was never very popular, either with guitarists or bassists, and the model was discontinued in 1975. A Japanese-made reissue was briefly available in the late 1990s.

Max Bennett, a musician's musician, gives son Adam, 3, some instruction on the finer points of the Fender bass. (See story, page 3.)

Max Bennett was another L.A. studio musician who adopted the Fender bass. Although he had early training on guitar, he had played the upright bass since high school. After buying a '62 Precision, Bennett discovered he could get more work—and have more fun doing it. "I immediately felt the electric was more versatile," he later explained. "It allowed me to be heard, so I could concentrate on what I was playing. Plus, after years of walking bass lines, I'd grown weary of traditional jazz forms. There were many more interesting rhythmic concepts happening on the electric."

Joltin' Joe

Joe Osborn was another key figure in the burgeoning Fender bass revolution. Like Carol Kaye, Osborn was a guitarist who had switched to bass, so playing his Fender bass with a pick came naturally to him—and it gave him an edge in the studio.

As Osborn told Chris Jisi, he became a bass player out of necessity: "Roy Buchanan and I were playing guitar in Bob Luhman's band at the

Showboat Hotel in Las Vegas in 1959. While we were there, we borrowed an electric bass and Roy started playing it, since Bob liked the way I played his country licks. Later, Bob added a female vocalist who sang a lot of pop standards; I didn't know all the chords, so I told Roy he'd have to come back to guitar. I went down to the local music store and bought a Precision Bass. The next night, I was the bass player—same amp, same settings, same pick and technique. I played it just like I played the guitar."

Osborn didn't think much of it at the time, but his approach gave him a distinct advantage over other bassists. "Eventually, I realized that my bass, played with the pick, had its own frequency space. Instead of competing with the kick drum at the very bottom, there was more of a blend. Plus it held up on any kind of record—even if the bass was EQ'd different, there was an attitude about it, a certain tone that you couldn't lose."

Joe's clear, distinct sound was greatly appreciated. He soon found steady work as the bassist in Ricky Nelson's band, where he was introduced to a new Fender model. "We were going on an Australian tour with Ricky in 1960, and Fender wanted us to take their equipment," Osborn recalled. "I asked for a Concert, which was their biggest amp, and a bass, thinking they made only the Precision. When they sent the Jazz Bass instead I was pretty annoyed, but I fell in love with it because the thinner neck was perfect for my short fingers."

Leo Fender had decided to keep the Precision as his only bass during the 1950s, preferring to modify and improve it rather than introduce an alternative model. (A '57 Precision Bass was quite different in almost every important way from its '51 predecessor, yet it still carried the same name.) In 1959, Leo finally changed his mind, probably with some prodding from the company's sales office.

The Fender Jazz Bass was developed in 1959 and introduced the following year. Its name is an interesting misnomer. It was probably intended to send the message that this new instrument was a "high-end" model for advanced players with jazz technique, because it had a slim neck that was narrow at the nut: only $1^7/_{16}$" compared to $1^3/_4$" on a Precision. Of course, most jazz musicians played the upright—which has a much *bigger* neck than the P-Bass. The Jazz Bass also had a more elaborate two-pickup configuration and a sleek, offset body shape. As it turned out, it would not be used by any notable jazz players for quite a few years, but it was adopted in other styles by bassists—including Joe Osborn.

Armed with his new Jazz Bass, Osborn quickly built a reputation as an innovative player who always got a great sound on tape. By 1963 he was a top L.A. session man, and he would contribute his distinctive tone and creative fills to a long string of hit songs by the Mamas & the Papas ("California Dreamin'," "Monday Monday"), the Carpenters ("Close to You," "We've Only Just Begun"), Johnny Rivers ("Memphis"), Glen Campbell ("Gentle on My Mind"), the Fifth Dimension ("Up, Up and Away"), Scott McKenzie ("San Francisco"), and many others. Joe also has the dubious distinction of having played his Hagstrom 8-string bass on Richard Harris's overblown version of "MacArthur Park." But that's another story.

By applying a pick—and considerable talent—to their Fender basses, Carol Kaye and Joe Osborn took a leading role in transforming the way popular music sounded. Rock & roll was coming of age, and the Fender bass was the catalyst in an explosive reaction between that nascent musical style and the lives of a generation just reaching their teen years at the dawn of the 1960s.

But there was one more key ingredient. Just as Kaye and Osborn were starting to send their low-end messages from California, the full range of expression made possible by the Fender bass was being revealed by a bassist working anonymously in a small studio in Detroit. His innovative playing on a series of hit records in the early '60s assured that this new instrument, barely ten years old, would play a huge role in the years to come.

Chapter 8: St. James

The commercial viability of the Fender bass was by no means guaranteed, even after ten years on the market. There are no precise records of Fender's Precision Bass production in the 1950s, but we know the numbers were low. According to Richard R. Smith, who has scrutinized the early Fender sales orders, it appears that fewer than 200 P-Basses were made each year in the early '50s, with a gradual increase to annual production of perhaps 1,000 by the end of the decade.

By 1961, a few players (most of them converted guitarists) had begun to define a sound and an approach that distinguished the Fender bass from the upright. But the instrument was awaiting its first virtuoso—the player who would expand the range of creative possibilities and firmly establish the position of the electric bass in the musical world. He would arrive in the form of an unassuming studio musician working for a fledgling record label in Detroit: James Jamerson.

Jamerson was a bass player, not a guitarist. After dabbling with the piano as a child, he studied acoustic bass in high school. He was a quick learner, and before long he was playing jazz on the upright and trying to emulate such heroes as Paul Chambers and Ray Brown. Jamerson's

James Jamerson played the bass lines for dozens of Motown hits on one instrument: a sunburst '62 Fender Precision Bass known as "the Funk Machine." The instrument was completely stock and still had its chrome pickup cover and bridge cover (with foam string mute) in place. The strings were LaBella flatwounds—the older and deader, the better. The action was very high, probably because of Jamerson's background on the upright. The bass was stolen shortly before Jamerson's death and has never been recovered.

After Leo Fender sold his company to CBS in January 1965, the new management introduced a number of unusual instruments, including this 5-string bass. It added a high *C* string to the usual *EADG* and had only 15 frets. James Jamerson owned a Bass V and may have experimented with it occasionally in the studio.

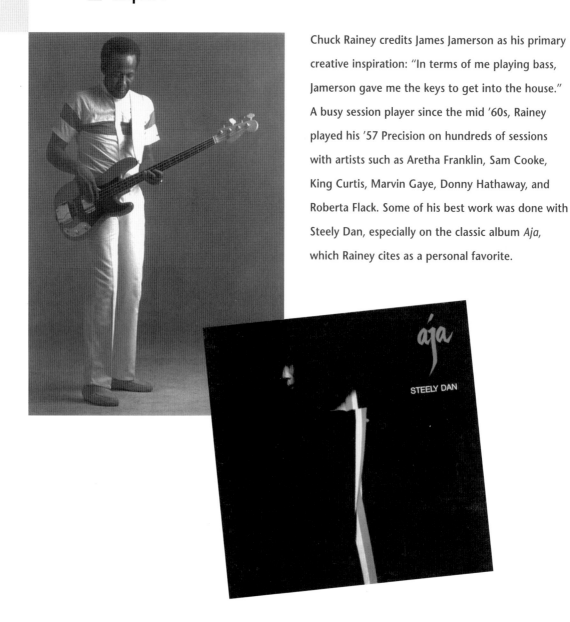

Chuck Rainey credits James Jamerson as his primary
creative inspiration: "In terms of me playing bass,
Jamerson gave me the keys to get into the house."
A busy session player since the mid '60s, Rainey
played his '57 Precision on hundreds of sessions
with artists such as Aretha Franklin, Sam Cooke,
King Curtis, Marvin Gaye, Donny Hathaway, and
Roberta Flack. Some of his best work was done with
Steely Dan, especially on the classic album *Aja*,
which Rainey cites as a personal favorite.

ability as a club musician came to the attention of several local producers, including Motown's Berry Gordy, and James began to get calls for
session work.

Jamerson started to work for Motown in 1959. He played his early sessions on the upright, but his approach was dramatically different from
that of the era's other bassists. Allan "Dr. Licks" Slutsky, the author of the
authoritative Jamerson biography, *Standing in the Shadows of Motown*,
described his impact: "Although his early Motown bass work was
nowhere near the mature late-'60s style that would ultimately evolve in

masterpieces like 'Bernadette' and 'I Was Made to Love Her,' James was quickly setting himself apart from most of the bassists in the R&B industry. Gone were the stagnant two-beat, root-fifth patterns and post-'Under the Boardwalk' clichéd bass lines that occupied the bottom end of most R&B releases. Jamerson had modified them or replaced them with chromatic passing tones, Ray Brown-style walking bass lines, and syncopated eighth-note figures—all of which had previously been unheard of in popular music in the late '50s and early '60s."

Sometime in 1961, Jamerson began to play a Fender Precision Bass. A friend and fellow bassist, Horace "Chili" Ruth, had urged him to try the new instrument. Resistant at first, James eventually decided he liked the Fender well enough to try it in the studio. Although Motown's studio records do not provide any definitive information, Slutsky says he believes that "Strange I Know" by the Marvellettes was probably the first Motown recording Jamerson made with a Fender bass. It was released in 1962.

The first track where you can hear Jamerson's unique style begin to emerge is Marvin Gaye's "Pride and Joy," which was released in April 1963. (It went to No. 2 on the R&B charts and No. 10 on the Pop charts.) The tune begins with a walking bass intro over handclaps, and the bass line under the verse is a standard blues pattern. Although simple, it's played with great feel, and there are subtle embellishments and accents that give the groove life and energy. For the final chorus, Jamerson returns to the walking line, playing it with a relaxed, infectious swing and tossing in surprising cross-string rakes and melodic fills. The entire part builds and develops, as if it were a two-minute bass concerto (and the singer isn't bad, either).

Jamerson's style continued to evolve, and Motown's producers gave him increasing freedom to shape his parts. He took full advantage of the opportunity, and by the mid '60s Jamerson had elevated pop bass playing to an art form. As Slutsky explained it: "Through 1965, James probably

While James Jamerson and his colleagues were making history in Detroit, another great rhythm section was doing groundbreaking work for Stax Records in Memphis. Duck Dunn was the bassist, and his name was better known than Jamerson's because the Stax rhythm section recorded on its own as Booker T. & the MG's. Dunn's stark, earthy lines are the driving force behind many great tracks by Otis Redding ("I've Been Loving You Too Long") and Sam & Dave ("Soul Man") as well as Booker T. instrumental hits like "Boot-Leg" and "Hip-Hug-Her."

A talented guitarist as well as bassist, Tommy Cogbill was a mainstay at the legendary Fame Studio in Muscle Shoals, Alabama, during the 1960s. His style blended Carol Kaye's studio savvy with Joe Osborn's great sound—and he had a deeper in-the-pocket feel than either of them. Cogbill's consistently inventive lines, played on a Precision Bass, propelled such hits as Aretha Franklin's "Respect" and Wilson Pickett's "The Land of 1,000 Dances" and "Funky Broadway."

Memphis Boys Mike Leech (second from left) and Tommy Cogbill (third from left) hangin' out in the studio with a Fender bass wannabe named Elvis.

Although the bassists changed regularly, the mid-'60s rhythm sections of James Brown set the standard for gutbucket grooves. Bernard Odum had one of the longest tenures and contributed to the recorded version of "Cold Sweat." Charles Sherrell, Tim Drummond, and Bootsy Collins also had significant stints with the Godfather of Soul. Their work has had an enduring influence on many styles, including contemporary hip-hop.

Like Booker T. & the MGs, the top late-'60s/early-'70s rhythm section in New Orleans also recorded under its own name. They were known as the Meters, and the bassist was the supremely funky George Porter Jr., whose potent lines anchored instrumentals like "Cissy Strut" and "Look-Ka Py Py." Porter's favorite basses included a Precision with a '70 body and a "'60-something" neck. He also used a Fender Telecaster Bass, a model introduced in 1968 that echoed the design of the original '51 Precision Bass.

Just about any Atlantic Records soul session from the late '60s that didn't have Chuck Rainey or Tommy Cogbill on bass featured the impeccable grooves of Jerry Jemmott on his '65 Jazz Bass. Jerry's work graced classic albums by Wilson Pickett, Aretha Franklin, King Curtis, B.B. King, and many others. In a 1984 interview, Jaco Pastorius said, "He was my idol, making the sounds I wanted to make."

had the funkiest and most melodic eighth-note bass style in the universe, but for some reason toward the end of the year, he exploded in a completely new direction. Sixteenth-notes, quarter-note triplets, open-string techniques, dissonant non-harmonic pitches, and syncopations off the 16th seemed to enter into his style almost overnight. It closely paralleled the change in the jazz world from Charlie Parker's eighth-note bebop style to the evolution of John Coltrane's 16th-note 'sheets of sound' approach. There is a distinct break from the bass lines Jamerson was playing in '64 and early '65 on tunes like 'Dancing in the Street' and 'Stop! In the Name of Love' to '66 and '67 masterpieces like 'Reach Out' and 'I'm Wondering.' Out of nowhere, James started playing almost as if he was the featured soloist."

Slutsky's book has transcriptions of 50 Jamerson bass lines, almost all of which are amazingly creative, even by contemporary standards. In a chapter called "An Appreciation of the Style," Anthony Jackson offers a detailed analysis of three songs, showing how Jamerson used unusual melodic and rhythmic devices to make his lines strong and distinctive. While influenced by Jamerson's knowledge of jazz, many of these ideas would be difficult to execute on the upright. They are truly *electric* bass lines, and they demonstrate the expressive capabilities of the instrument. "Perhaps the key word that sums up [Jamerson's] techniques," wrote Jackson, "is unpredictability. It was impossible to foresee what he would

David Hood and drummer Roger Hawkins have been the backbone of the Muscle Shoals studio rhythm section for more than 30 years. Hood, who began his career playing a '61 Jazz Bass, has nailed the groove with everyone from Wilson Pickett to the Staple Singers to Paul Simon.

play." In contrast to the formulaic bass playing in pop music before then, Jamerson's work was a revelation.

And, because it was a vital component of a long string of hit records, Jamerson's playing reached the ears (and feet) of millions. It helped to break down the line that supposedly separated "Pop" (white) music from "R&B" (black) music. It is not an exaggeration to say that the immense popularity of Motown changed the course of American popular music and, in doing so, had a huge impact on the development of an entire generation. Certainly, there were many reasons for Motown's success—from Smokey Robinson's voice to Berry Gordy's business savvy—but much credit must go to James Jamerson and his '62 Precision Bass (known as "The Funk Machine"), as well as his colleagues in the great rhythm section known collectively as the Funk Brothers.

It is hugely ironic—and there were many ironies in Jamerson's life—that all of this happened without anyone knowing who this great bass player was. (Motown, like many other labels of that era, did not list the backing musicians on its records.) James finally received a credit in 1971, on Marvin Gaye's *What's Going On*, a landmark album that broke all of Motown's sales records.

Veteran Chicago bassist Jerome Arnold was a founding member of the Paul Butterfield Blues Band. The strong, punchy tone of his Jazz Bass was a key ingredient in the success of the band's 1965 debut album, which took the exciting sound of the amplified Chicago blues bands to a wide audience.

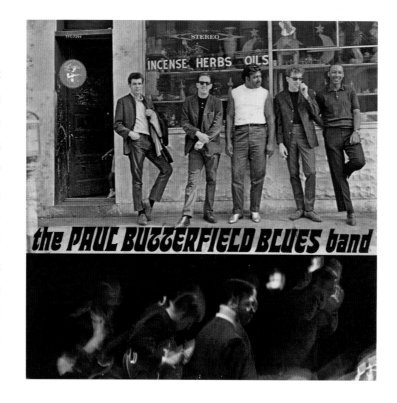

But it would be years before Jamerson would be properly acknowledged for his accomplishments. Plagued by alcoholism and self-doubt, victimized by the shifting fortunes of the music industry, he died lonely and embittered in 1983. Years later, his Motown colleague Smokey Robinson paid tribute to him, saying: "He's really the father of the modern-day bass player. He had the purest fingering—all his notes were pure and true. No matter how fast he was playing them or whatever rhythmic pattern he was doing, you could hear the whole note. That was a big part of his sound. Even today, nobody plays like that."

Although he was known for many years only as "the Motown bass player" (or "the Tamla bass player," as the label was named on U.K. releases), Jamerson was highly influential among his fellow bassists. Now that we know his name, he has taken on the status of a patron saint—a player inspired by a vision of his instrument's potential whose work showed the way to those who followed, and who shared his gift in a selfless and almost self-sacrificing way.

Bob Babbitt began to do session work at Motown in 1967 as a "pinch hitter" for James Jamerson. He eventually contributed to dozens of hits by artists such as Stevie Wonder, the Temptations, Gladys Knight, and Marvin Gaye. His favorite recording bass for many years was a modified mid-'60s Precision.

As James Jamerson developed his virtuosic style in the early 1960s, there was a young English musician who listened closely and began to seek his own distinctive electric bass approach. While he was different in just about every important way from "the Tamla bass player," this left-handed guitarist-turned-bassist was perhaps the most gifted member of a rock & roll band whose popularity has never been exceeded—and whose creative influence is still powerful today.

Chapter 9: All You Need Is Bass

Paul McCartney found the symmetrical Hofner 500/1 bass appealing because he was left-handed; the right-handed Hofner didn't look odd when he turned it over to play lefty. He also liked it because it was "so light you play it a bit like a guitar—all that high trilling stuff I used to do…was because of the Hofner."

If James Jamerson was the first player to reveal that the electric bass had unique creative possibilities, then Paul McCartney made sure *everyone* got the message. Thanks to his position as the bassist in the most popular group in the history of rock & roll, Paul had a platform for making a statement that would influence countless listeners, musicians and non-musicians alike. And he made the most of it.

In 1961, the Beatles were a fledgling quintet with Stu Sutcliffe on bass. John, George, and Paul all played guitar. After Sutcliffe quit the band to focus on his painting (a bad career move, to be sure), Paul was drafted to play bass—mostly because his cheap guitar was broken. He adapted quickly and soon discovered that he rather enjoyed his new instrument. "I'd always liked bass," McCartney told Tony Bacon, "[and] then I started listening to other bass players—mainly Motown. As time went on, James Jamerson became my hero, although I didn't actually know his name until quite recently."

It's worth noting that McCartney is the first important "Fender bassist" in this saga who didn't play a bass made by Fender. One reason was money: Fender instruments were quite expensive as imports, and Paul refused to go into debt to buy one. He was also left-handed. Left-handed production basses were rare in the early '60s, and most right-handed models looked and felt odd when flipped over and restrung for southpaw playing. McCartney found the solution in an inexpensive German-made bass, as he explained to Tom Mulhern in 1990: "The Hofner [500/1 bass] was violin-shaped and symmetrical, so being left-handed didn't look so stupid. And once I bought it, I fell in love with it." The Hofner became Paul's signature instrument, and he used the axe now commonly called a "Beatle Bass" almost exclusively until he received a left-handed Rickenbacker bass in 1965.

With Paul getting more comfortable on bass and the songwriting team of Lennon and McCartney churning out one memorable song after another, the Beatles captured the hearts and minds of an entire generation. To grasp the incredible impact they had on popular music in the early 1960s, all you have to do is glance at the *Billboard* charts for 1963 and 1964 (see charts, page 84). A year after music lovers had been flocking to stores to pick up 45s of "Sugar Shack" and "Dominique," they were bowled over by "I Want to Hold Your Hand" and "Can't Buy Me Love"—and the Beatles had *seven* more songs in the Top 40 of 1964. The syrupy pop confections of the late 1950s had been completely displaced by an exciting new style propelled by the electric bass. And rock & roll was more than entertainment—it was becoming

Rickenbacker presented Paul McCartney with a left-handed 4001S in 1965. It eventually became his main bass, and he used it to record *Sgt. Pepper's Lonely Hearts Club Band*. Originally Fireglo Red, the Rick got a psychedelic paint job for Magical Mystery Tour and was later refinished natural.

a social force that united its fans and gave them a new system of shared values and beliefs.

A Style Is Born

Paul McCartney's early bass work was solid if unremarkable, but by early 1964 the influence of James Jamerson began to show in lines that were becoming more and more melodic and rhythmically adventurous. One of the best places to trace this development is on *Live at the BBC*, a two-CD collection of early Beatles recordings made for radio broadcast by the British Broadcasting Corporation. Recorded between 1963 and 1965, the tracks provide a wonderful cross-section of the group's progress during that period. As you listen to these quickly recorded live performances, you can hear Paul moving away from the simple bass patterns he had learned from early R&B and country music and beginning to develop the melodic, contrapuntal style that would soon become his trademark.

The tracks on these CDs are not arranged in chronological order, so it takes some effort to trace the evolution of McCartney's style. On the earliest cuts, such as "Keep Your Hands Off My Baby" (January 1963), the bass playing is rudimentary: Paul's sound is blurry, and he sticks to root-fifth patterns broken up by the simplest of fills. Even so, you can tell he has a good feel for bass playing, and the other instrumental parts, even at this point, seem to hinge on his lines. Within a few months, Paul's lines progress further, and he occasionally breaks up the root-fifth tedium with walking lines and pumping triadic figures.

McCartney's bass playing really began to blossom as the Beatles wrote more original material. The BBC version of "I Saw Her Standing There" (October 1963) is a big step forward: Paul's playing is more imaginative and has terrific rhythmic vitality. And on a January 1964 cover of "Johnny B. Goode," we hear a bass line that develops continually throughout the song, becoming more and more complex without ever losing the groove—a characteristic of many great James Jamerson lines.

Everything comes together on the version of "All My Loving" the Beatles recorded at the Piccadilly Theatre, London, on February 28, 1964. The walking line under the verses is surprisingly sophisticated (especially since Paul is singing the lead vocal), and the bass line just *drives* the band. It's essentially the same part McCartney had played on the studio version of the song (recorded six months earlier), but his performance on this live track is much more confident and prominent in the mix. It was a sure sign of the greatness that was to come.

In addition to having a great ear and a sure sense of rhythm, Paul was blessed with a spirit of adventure. He was ready to try almost anything in a bass line. "As time went on, I began to realize you didn't have to play just the root notes," he explained. "If [the chords were] C, F, and G, then it was normally C, F, and G that I played. But I started to realize you could be pulling on the G, or just stay on the C when it went to F. And then I took it beyond that. I thought, Well, if you can do that, what else could you do, how much further could you take it? You might even be able to play notes that aren't in the chord."

While Bill Wyman of the Rolling Stones lacked Paul McCartney's creative gift, he was a reliable bass player who always seemed to find the right feel for each song. Small in stature, Wyman favored short-scale basses, including the Fender Mustang. Fender introduced the budget-priced Mustang in 1966 as an alternative to the long-scale Precision and Jazz models.

McCartney credits the Beach Boys' Brian Wilson as an inspiration in this area. "With the Beach Boys, the band might be playing in *C*," Paul explained, "but the bass might stay on the *G* just to hold it all back. I started to realize the power the bass player had within the band." Paul took this idea even further, and many of the lines he played during the Beatles' great creative outburst of 1965 to 1967—when they recorded *Rubber Soul, Revolver,* and *Sgt. Pepper's Lonely Hearts Club Band*—go well beyond Wilson's most creative bass parts.

"Michelle," recorded in November 1965, is an excellent example of McCartney's burgeoning creative approach. Paul recalled the moment this way: "That was actually thought up on the spot. That opening six-note phrase against the descending chords in 'Michelle'—that was like, oh, a great moment in my life. I think I had enough musical experience after years of playing, so it was just in me. I realized I could do that." Paul's experience as a lead guitarist, limited though it was, was undoubtedly helpful, and his best bass lines combine the traditional support function of bass with the freedom and lyricism of great lead-guitar lines.

McCartney was given a left-handed Rickenbacker 4001S in 1965, and he began to use that bass along with his trusty Hofner. By the time *Sgt. Pepper* was recorded in 1967, the Rick had become his primary instrument. By then, his playing had progressed to the point where he felt confident enough to try some radical experiments. "I was thinking that maybe I could even run a little tune through the chords that doesn't exist anywhere else. Maybe I can have an independent melody? *Sgt. Pepper* ended up being my strongest thing on bass—the independent melodies. On 'Lucy in the Sky with Diamonds,' for example, you could easily have had root notes, whereas I was running an independent melody through it, and that became my thing. It's really only a way of getting from *C* to *F* or whatever, but you get there in an interesting way. So once I got over the fact that I was lumbered with bass, I did get quite proud to be a bass player. It was all very exciting…. As it went on and got into that melodic thing, that was probably the peak of my interest."

In fact, if you had to chose a single recording that proved the electric bass had reached maturity, then *Sgt. Pepper* would be it. The music on that classic album simply would not have worked without Paul McCartney's exceptional artistry, which was highlighted by production that put the sound of his bass front and center. As Abbey Road engineer Geoff Emerick later explained to Howard Massey, the bass on *Sgt. Pepper* was isolated on its own track and recorded simply by miking the bass amp rather than using direct input (DI) or a mix of amp plus DI. "Although he changed from the Hofner to the Rickenbacker at around that time, I don't think it was so much the bass guitar he used," said Emerick. "I think it was having the mike on figure 8 [pickup pattern]. With the studio empty, you could actually hear a little bit of the room ambience around the bass, which seemed to help… The other thing I used to do when I was mixing—and [previous Beatles engineer] Norman Smith taught me this—was that the last instrument that you bring in is the bass. So, at least through *Pepper*, everything was mixed without hearing the bass. I used to bring everything to –2 on the VU meter and then bring the bass in and make it go to 0, so it meant the bass was 2dB louder than anything on the record; it was way out in front, the loudest thing on the record."

McCartney's brilliance, augmented by sympathetic production (and improved recording technology), had given the bass the dominant role on the most important rock recording of the 1960s. Sixteen years after Leo Fender had decided he wanted to free bass players from "the big doghouse," his new instrument had completely transformed popular music.

You Say You Want a Revolution?

Top 10 Hits of 1963

1. "Sugar Shack" by Jimmy Gilmer & the Fireballs
2. "He's So Fine" by the Chiffons
3. "Dominique" by the Singing Nun
4. "Hey Paula" by Paul & Paula
5. "My Boyfriend's Back" by the Angels
6. "Blue Velvet" by Bobby Vinton
7. "Sukiyaki" by Kyu Sakamoto
8. "I Will Follow Him" by Little Peggy March
9. "Fingertips, Pt. 2" by Little Stevie Wonder
10. "Walk Like a Man" by the Four Seasons

Top 10 Hits of 1964

1. "I Want to Hold Your Hand" by the Beatles
2. "Can't Buy Me Love" by the Beatles
3. "There! I've Said It Again" by Bobby Vinton
4. "Baby Love" by the Supremes
5. "Oh, Pretty Woman" by Roy Orbison
6. "The House of the Rising Sun" by the Animals
7. "Chapel of Love" by the Dixie Cups
8. "I Feel Fine" by the Beatles
9. "She Loves You" by the Beatles
10. "I Get Around" by the Beach Boys

Chapter 10: The Big Boing

In a special issue of *Time* magazine titled "Artists & Entertainers of the Century" (June 8, 1998), Executive Editor Christopher Porterfield offered an analysis of the effect of technology on the arts in the twentieth century. He noted two great "convulsions," one caused by World War I and the other by the 1960s. Of the latter, he wrote: "Again, a rupture opened with the past; received standards and values were under siege, this time in the ferment of civil rights, the sexual revolution, and Vietnam. In the arts the rumbling had started in the '50s, when Elvis Presley got everybody all shook up, when Jack Kerouac took to the road, and Allen Ginsberg began to howl. In 1969, in a muddy field in New York's Catskill Mountains, more than 400,000 of their spiritual heirs gathered at the Woodstock Festival to stake their claim as a new generation and a new social and political force, complete with a language of their own—rock music."

The maturation of rock as an important musical and social force is directly linked to the acceptance of the electric bass. The other crucial rock instruments—the electric guitar and the drum kit—had been around for decades, but the "new bass," which changed the way rhythm sections

An experienced session musician before he was tapped to play bass in Led Zeppelin, John Paul Jones was a powerful creative force in the band, writing many of their best-known riffs and holding everything together with a beloved Fender Jazz Bass he had purchased in 1963.

Throughout his long career, John Entwistle has played (and collected) dozens of different instruments, from stock Precision Basses to the exotic all-graphite Status Buzzard. For a time he favored "Fenderbirds": unique instruments he created by attaching a Precision Bass neck to a Gibson Thunderbird Bass body.

worked and altered the dynamic contours of popular music, was the last piece of the puzzle. Without it, there would have been no Beatles, no Rolling Stones—and no Woodstock.

Tommy, Can You Hear Me?

One of the most spectacular performances at the 1969 Woodstock Festival was the early-morning show by the Who. As the sun rose on 400,000 of Elvis's spiritual heirs, the British band that had once been known as the High Numbers put on a powerful show featuring many of the songs from their recently released rock opera, *Tommy*. Holding it all together, and playing bass in a highly original and unusual style, was John Entwistle.

As Chris Jisi has noted, John is "hardly a proper bassist at all; more accurately, Entwistle is one of the first bass guitarists to play the instru-

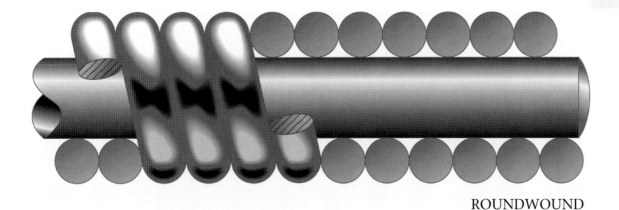

ROUNDWOUND

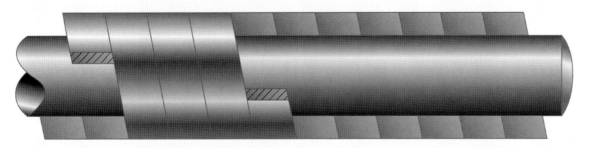

FLATWOUND

ment so improperly that through his own sheer aggression, technique, and sonic vision, the spare setting of his three-piece [plus vocalist] always seemed far, far larger."

Because he played in a band with Pete Townshend, a guitarist whose style was primarily chordal, Entwistle was free to develop a busy, melodic "lead bass" style. Influenced by the twanging guitar of Duane Eddy, he sought a bright, penetrating sound that would allow him to play a lot of notes and still be heard over the din of Townshend's amps and Keith Moon's bombastic drumming. "What I didn't realize was that I'd set quite a task for myself," he told Jisi, "because you can't play sloppily using that much high end. I had to clean it up and find a fluid way of damping the notes so they didn't blur into each other or vary in volume."

Entwistle's other problem was strings. In 1965, when he set out to record the first notable rock-bass solo on "My Generation," he wanted as

The first strings manufactured for the Fender Precision Bass were steel flatwounds. In 1963, James How created his Rotosound JS66 design by using a round outer wrap instead of a flat one. Although more abrasive, the new strings had a brilliant tone that no flatwound could match—and they changed the way basses were built and played.

The bright, aggressive tone Chris Squire perfected in Yes was highly influential in the early 1970s. Squire used a Rickenbacker 4001S, equipped with Rotosound roundwound strings and played with a pick, to get a bass sound that would have been unimaginable only a few years before.

bright a sound as possible. His first choice was a Danelectro bass. "We did three takes," John recalled, "all of which were faster, more trebly, and more complex than the final one, and I kept breaking strings. You couldn't get replacements, so I had to keep buying Danelectros. When the store finally ran out of them, I bought a Fender Jazz Bass, put on LaBella strings, and used it to cut the final version."

Those were LaBella *flatwound* strings, of course. Although a brand-new set had worked well enough on "My Generation," they simply weren't intended to produce the kind of razor-edged, trebly tone Entwistle wanted. He soon found what he needed in an all-new type of bass string.

The String Thing

Strings are often overlooked in discussions of the development of stringed instruments, but they are an absolutely critical component of tone production. Many of the different approachs to constructing and tuning the earliest bass instruments (see Chapter 1) were attempts to overcome the shortcomings of the strings. A 3-string acoustic upright bass tuned *ADG* seems odd to us today, but it was popular in the eighteenth century because the *E* strings of the time were so bad. The science of string-

making had not progressed sufficiently to produce an *E* string that possessed the clarity and power of the other three.

There isn't a lot of information about ancient strings. We know that the history of stringed instruments can be traced back to the lyres of ancient Greece, but we're not sure what the earliest strings were made of—probably horsehair, silk, and other organic materials. The first important breakthrough in string technology occurred when someone discovered that the intestines of sheep could be used to make better-sounding strings. According to legend, this happened in Italy during the Middle Ages; strands of sheep gut were used for sewing leather, and a musically inclined saddler must have plucked a taut strand one day and liked what he heard.

Before long, gut became the standard material for stringing lutes, violins, and other instruments. It works well for that purpose, especially when gut strands are woven like rope into "catlines." The problem with making bass strings this way is that you need a lot of mass to produce low notes and still maintain a workable string tension, so the strings must be large. This makes them hard to play and somewhat indistinct in tone. The

When Jimi Hendrix asked guitarist Noel Redding to play bass in the Experience, Redding asked John Entwistle for advice. "He rang me up and asked what kind of equipment I used," recalled John, "which was a Jazz Bass, Rotosounds, and Marshalls, so that's what he went for." Redding made his bass-playing debut on the incredible 1967 album *Are You Experienced?*, which included "Foxy Lady," "Purple Haze," "Manic Depression," and "The Wind Cries Mary."

solution to this dilemma was discovered around 1650, with the development of the overwound string. Someone figured out that you could increase the mass of a gut string by winding metal wire over the outside; for basses, this yielded a thinner string with a more musical tone than that of a thick, all-gut string. Overwound strings were soon adopted for many instruments, and they paved the way for the establishment of the *EADG*-tuned 4-string as the standard orchestral bass.

Overwound strings have improved a lot since the seventeenth century, but the basic design concept remains the same: a core string (usually made of gut, nylon, silk, or steel) is wrapped with one or more layers of metal wire. The materials, the dimensions of the wire, the winding tension, and other factors can be varied to produce different musical results.

The strings used today on many uprights have a final wind of flat metal tape, which produces a smooth playing surface that responds well to the bow. The first strings designed for the electric bass followed this model—although, as former Fender executive Forrest White has noted, strings were an impediment to Leo Fender's early experiments: "Strings for the prototype electric basses did not exist because there were no instruments to put them on…. Leo had to take gut strings [for upright bass] and wrap them with small-gauge iron wire for his first units. He said this was a heck of a job. Of course, after the bass proved successful, he had V.C. Squier make the strings for him." (Squier was a string-manufacturing company Fender later acquired.)

The early Fender bass strings were heavy-gauge flatwounds that were easy on the fingers and produced a solid fundamental, although their tone was dull and one-dimensional. There was little change to this basic design during the 1950s and early 1960s. Then, in 1963, an English string-maker named James How had a better idea: the roundwound bass string. Rather than putting on a final winding of flat metal tape, he used round nickel-steel wire, which produced a much brighter sound (although it was hard on the frets and the bassist's fingers).

The new Rotosound "Swing Bass" strings were exactly what John Entwistle was looking for, and he became one of the company's most enthusiastic product-development consultants. ("After each concert...I visited the Rotosound factory and had them make me sets until they came up with what I was looking for.") Armed with the crisper, brighter tone of Rotosounds, Entwistle was able to push his sound even more to the forefront—something that did not go unnoticed among his fellow bassists.

One of the players who was heavily influenced by the "big boing" of John Entwistle's sound was Chris Squire. He had co-founded the British progressive band Yes in 1968 and was looking for a different way to play bass, a style that would make the bass equally as important as the other instruments in the band. "I had always played with a pick because I hated the dull, boomy tone most bassists had," Squire told Chris Jisi. "John was using a pick [the first time I saw him]—and his massive cutting sound and integral parts were inspirational."

Equipped with a Rickenbacker 4001S bass strung with Rotosound roundwounds—and often plugged into a guitar amp for added treble response—Squire took the "lead bass" concept to new heights. When the Yes song "Roundabout" became a hit in 1972, Squire's bright, "spring-like" sound reached millions of listeners and transfixed countless young bassists. A similar development was taking place across the Atlantic, where a pair of American bass players were helping to define the "San Francisco Sound" as they rewrote the rules for rock bass playing.

Chapter 11: S.F. Giants

Early in his career, Jack Casady played a Fender Jazz Bass. He recorded the first two Jefferson Airplane albums with a J-Bass before switching to a short-scale Guild Starfire.

Whether or not there was ever such a thing as a San Francisco sound, there certainly was a Jack Casady sound. As Chris Jisi put it, the electric bass "underwent one of its most radical transformations in San Francisco in the hands of Jack Casady. Casady did far more than provide a solid runway for the improvisational folk-rock flights of Jefferson Airplane. With his innovative use of spontaneous upper-register melodies, dramatic overdriven chords, and thunderous low-end bursts, Jack was the Airplane's pilot, navigator, and bombardier all at once."

Casady started his career as a guitarist, emulating such early rock & roll heroes as Chuck Berry, Gene Vincent, and Buddy Holly. After encountering a Precision Bass at a nightclub, he began to double on bass. Discovering that he could get more work as a bassist than a guitarist (one of the eternal economic realities of the music business), Casady bought a Fender Jazz Bass. In 1965, he took the J-Bass with him when he left Washington, D.C., to go to San Francisco to become a member of the Jefferson Airplane, at the invitation of guitarist Jorma Kaukonen.

Jack Casady's Guild basses were heavily modified by Ron Wickersham of Alembic, who installed active electronics designed to produce a more even sound with improved high-frequency response.

Like Paul McCartney and John Entwistle, Casady believed the bass should play a prominent role in rock music. "The nature of the bass," he has explained, "is to work with and support the other instruments in a dialogue." For Casady, that meant playing strong melodic lines that were often the focal point of the songs, much as McCartney's lines on *Sgt. Pepper* had been. Jack's playing on the first two Airplane albums, *Jefferson Airplane Takes Off* and *Surrealistic Pillow*, hinted at this approach, but it was his work on *After Bathing at Baxter's*, *Crown of Creation*, and the live tour-de-force, *Bless Its Pointed Little Head*, that established him as a major bass innovator. Listening to Casady on those albums, wrote Dan Schwartz, "you hear bass as an equal voice, supportive and contrapuntal, painting with huge swatches of deep chords, limning the landscape with melodies and countermelodies, hammering down the bottom with pedal points of gigantic scale. And yet, at the same time, you hear a stunning delicacy, an intimacy with the instrument and the music with which that huge presence would seem to be completely at odds."

The Fender Bassman of the early '60s was the best bass amp of its time. The tube head sent 50 watts of power into a separate 2x12 cabinet, producing a bass sound with more clarity than anything else on the market.

Casady's style was so powerful because he focused on sound as much as technique—and the technology of the time was beginning to reach a point where it could offer him the power and clarity he needed to fully express his ideas. The first key to Casady's thundering late-'60s tone was a different instrument. He had used the Jazz Bass on the first two Airplane albums, but then he began to experiment with a semi-hollow Guild Starfire bass. "I noticed that the Fender didn't distort well," Casady explained, "but when I played overdriven chords and moved up the neck on the Guild, it had a sweet sustain with a lot of interesting overtones. Because it sang so well but lacked in the low end, due to its short scale, I found myself playing more melodically and higher on the neck."

The other ingredient in Casady's sonic recipe was an unusual amplifier called a Versatone. Originally designed to get a clean sound for acoustic bass, the 40-watts-per-channel Versatone found a different application with Casady. He explained: "It had separate tube amps for the highs and the lows—sort of an early version of bi-amping, except that both signals were sent through a single speaker. The mix of the highs and the lows was controlled by turning a PAN-O-FLEX knob. I plugged in and played, and it had a warm, round tone. When I turned up the volume to overdrive it, the amp put out a pleasant, smooth distortion instead of just breaking up. And when I turned it all the way up, it growled! Best of all, I was still getting the clean fundamental lows in addition to the dirty highs. I proceeded to record with it on a separate track for *Baxter's* and then used it all over *Crown of Creation*. On the live album, I had it miked separately from the rest of my amps and applied it like an effect with a volume pedal."

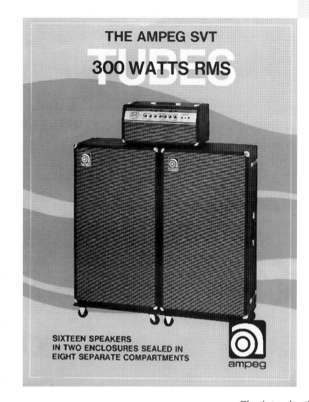

The introduction of the Ampeg SVT in 1969 marked the dawn of the modern era in bass amp technology. With its 300-watt head and dual 8x10 cabinets, the SVT could keep up with any guitar stack on the market.

Jack Casady used a Versatone—originally designed as an amplifier for acoustic bass—as a preamp. (The Versatone is sitting on the stage, right behind Casady's legs, in this photo.) Casady said he found its "smooth distortion" perfect for adding the right amount of edge to his tone.

Phil Lesh of the Grateful Dead had a totally original concept of how an electric bass should sound and how it should be played. Like Jack Casady, he was assisted by the wizards of Alembic in his efforts to get better sound from his gear.

Big Bottom

In addition to demonstrating what a creative player he was, the huge bass sound of Jack Casady showed how far bass amplification had advanced since 1951, when Leo Fender introduced the first Bassman amp. Before Leo, all of the attempts to create an electric bass instrument—vertical or horizontal—had fallen short because of inadequate amplification. Several of the primitive "stick" basses of the 1930s were sold with companion amplifiers, but these units were underpowered and their speakers ill-suited to reproducing low-frequency sounds. Paul Tutmarc's ground-breaking Model 736 Electronic Bass had a Model 936 amplifier to go with it, but that unit, too, was small and low-powered.

The slow acceptance of the Fender bass in the 1950s was due, at least in part, to the continuing inadequacy of bass amps. The original Fender Bassman worked fairly well at low volumes but was prone to speaker failures (which is one reason why Leo Fender kept tinkering with the design of the P-Bass pickup, looking for a way to soften the attack transient). An improved version was introduced in the mid '50s, with more power and a 4x10 speaker configuration. It was one of the keys to Joe Osborn's great studio sound but was still too weak for loud rock & roll performances. (On bass, anyway—guitarists loved it.)

In the early 1960s, Leo Fender found a better solution: a "piggyback" Bassman consisting of a separate head and speaker cabinet. The tube amplifier offered 50 watts of power, and the 2x12 cabinet held heavy-duty speakers that could handle the attack of notes played on electric bass. As David Hicks noted in *Bass Player*, "all of a sudden, you could *hear* the bass guitar, without a lot of buzz or distortion. At the time, it was the ultimate in bass gear."

Bass amps continued to get larger and more powerful throughout the '60s. The Beatles used 100-watt Vox amplifiers on their 1965 U.S. tour, with Paul McCartney's bass booming out of a "massive" (for the time) speaker cabinet with one 12" and one 15" speaker. Vox later licensed the Thomas Organ Company of California to produce solid-state Super Beatle amps that sent an 240 watts of "peak power" into 4x12 cabinets. The amplifier wars were under way.

Another California company, Acoustic Control, soon produced the first high-powered amp designed especially for bass performance. The Acoustic 360 had a 200-watt RMS solid-state power amp mounted in the bottom of a huge folded-horn enclosure with a single 18" speaker. The separate head was a preamp, with such unusual features as a built-in fuzztone and a VARIAMP control that was, in effect, a crude parametric equalizer. The cabinet design was something of a problem for bass players because it projected the sound so well it was hard to hear onstage. It was also a chore to move around. (In addition to being a powerful social force, rock & roll also may have inspired the invention of the van.) Despite its shortcomings, the Acoustic 360 was the first high-quality amplifier to offer bass players the volume they needed to keep up with Marshall guitar amps.

Fender followed suit with the 400 PS, another bulky two-piece stack with a folded-horn cabinet loaded with a single 18. The power amp was an all-tube unit that produced an astounding 440 watts RMS—and weighed nearly 100 pounds. Bass players were getting a stronger sound, but they needed to be physically stronger (or have sympathetic bandmates) just to drag their amps onstage.

Ampeg, under the leadership of bassist Everett Hull, had been one of the first companies to address amplification for acoustic basses, starting in the late 1940s. The product that launched the company was a microphone that could be installed inside a bass through the endpin (or peg) hole—thus "amp(lified) peg." In the '50s, Ampeg offered a line of bass amps, including one with 40 watts of power and two 15" speakers. Then, in 1960, the company introduced the famous B-15 Portaflex, the great-sounding favorite of James Jamerson and many other studio bassists—but it produced only 25 watts.

In response to the Acoustic 360, Ampeg upped the ante by creating a bass amp called the SVT. Introduced in 1969, it offered tons of power and an innovative cabinet design that proved to be the best solution for stage sound. The 300-watt RMS tube head was designed to drive two large closed-box cabinets, each loaded with eight 10" speakers. Ampeg's engineers had (correctly) figured that multiple small speakers working together could not only move enough air to get a good bass sound but would respond more quickly (have better "transient response") and offer crisper sound reproduction than larger speakers. This foreshadowed the many 2x10 and 4x10 cabinets available today. Original SVT amps are still in use, and the model, in many variations, remains the mainstay of Ampeg's bass amplifier line.

So, by 1970, the volume problem had largely been solved: well-made, high-powered amps and good electric bass guitars were available to any bass player (or, at least, to any bass player who could afford them). The technological limitations that had slowed the progress of the electric bass—and limited its influence—had largely disappeared.

Sound Refinement

Jack Casady's use of the Versatone amp pointed to another important aspect of the development of better bass tone: the application of superior electronics *before* the amp. Casady was using the Versatone as a separate preamp, taking advantage of its "smooth distortion" to give his sound presence and bite that would have been impossible before then. While Casady was conducting his research, another group of San Francisco musicians was also seeking a sonic edge by upgrading their gear.

Formed in 1965, the Grateful Dead immediately took an experimental approach to its music, combining elements of folk songs and early rock with psychedelicized jams inspired by the free jazz of John Coltrane and Ornette Coleman. Their bassist was Phil Lesh, a trumpet player who had been trained as a composer of modern classical music. Given his background, it wasn't surprising that Lesh took an unusual and highly individual approach to playing bass, one that featured long melodic lines that ran over, under, and through the music and often strayed far from the traditional bass function of harmonic and rhythmic support.

Like Casady, Lesh was obsessed with finding a better sound. "I wanted more tone out of the bass," he told Karl Coryat, "and I wanted to be able to boost any area of the frequency spectrum. But most of all, I wanted the tone to be consistent across the instrument's whole range." Phil was assisted in his efforts by Ron Wickersham of Alembic, a think tank of experts that worked with the Dead to improve their instruments and sound systems. (The name "alembic" means "anything that refines or purifies.")

The first Alembic bass was built for Jack Casady in 1971. It featured neck-through-body construction, active electronics, brass hardware, an inlaid ebony fingerboard, and a level of woodworking artistry never before seen in an electric bass. (The body was originally topped with bird's-eye maple plates, but they were later replaced with purpleheart.)

Alembic had been started in 1969, when Augustus Stanley Owsley invited Wickersham to become the Dead's electronic consultant. ("Bear" Owsley was a close associate of the band and reputedly the maker of the best LSD in San Francisco.) Wickersham had a background in radio and TV as well as experience as a recording engineer, and he had already been working with Bay Area musicians on improving the sound of their gear. When luthier Rick Turner and recording engineer Bob Matthews joined Wickersham, the Dead had assembled a remarkable group of "mad scientists" dedicated to sonic R&D.

Lesh's Guild Starfire was a focal point for Alembic's research. In search of the consistent tone Lesh wanted, Wickersham conducted numerous experiments and installed active electronics—the first time that had ever been done in an electric instrument. (Active electronics involve circuitry built into an instrument and usually powered by one or more onboard batteries.) Wickersham also modified Jack Casady's Guild bass, which was renamed "Mission Control" in honor of the array of knobs and switches that controlled the electronics. Wickersham's goal was to balance the sound from top to bottom—always a problem with bass guitars—and to reduce the high-frequency loss that occurs when signals travel from passive pickups through long guitar cords.

The next logical step for Alembic was designing and building a bass that embodied all of their ideas about both woodworking and electronics. "We postulated that the strings should be isolated from the body of the instrument," noted Wickersham, "as opposed to an acoustic instrument,

Perhaps in response to the popularity of the Guild Starfire, Fender introduced its own semi-hollow bass. A product of the notorious late-'60s period when the CBS management was seemingly intent on ruining the company's reputation, the Coronado Bass is usually seen as little more than a footnote in the history of the Fender bass—but it was created by Roger Rossmeisl, the luthier who had designed the Rickenbacker 4000, and the instrument has found some favor with roots rockers who like its thumpy sound.

where the string energy is coupled to the plates [vibrating surfaces] to produce the acoustic output, since sustain could be enhanced by reflecting energy back into the string rather than losing it to the body. So we placed a mass block under the bridge, which has the desired effect. Further, the traditional plastic or bone nut provided a different termination to an open string compared to the metal of a fret, so a brass nut was fitted. And we felt that better support for the string would be provided by a stiff neck extending through the body, so losses from friction at the neck joint would be eliminated."

The first Alembic bass was a truly revolutionary instrument and the most important new bass design since Leo Fender had created the Precision. It took the neck-through-body construction that had originated with the Rickenbacker 4000 and added laminated hardwoods, brass hardware, intricate inlays, and an elaborate electronics configuration that featured several sets of interchangable pickups mounted on sliding rails. Casady used it for several years until it was dropped on a concrete floor, causing body cracks that, according to Jack, ruined its tone.

Before the first Alembic bass, electric bass guitars had been utilitarian instruments—sometimes dressed up with "custom colors," perhaps, but still quite plain when compared to guitar makers' finest efforts. But Alembic's team changed everything. Not only did they bring a much more scientific approach to the design and installation of electronics, they created instruments that were often works of art. The Alembic legacy is much in evidence today; a display of basses at any large music store will have many beautiful, well-crafted instruments made of exotic woods and equipped with sophisticated active electronics.

In the same way, the influence of Casady and Lesh stretched far beyond the San Francisco scene. Their success in elevating bass playing to a new level of artistry enhanced the impact of the Airplane and the Dead, inspiring not only their fellow bassists but the many young adherents who were finding that "language of their own" in rock music. In the late

'60s, the United States was a country in turmoil, bitterly divided by controversies over political power, civil rights, and the Vietnam War. For the youth, rock was a rallying point in their struggle to influence the future direction of the country against the entrenched forces of "the Establishment." While many bands offered anthems for this crusade, the Jefferson Airplane might have summed it up best on their 1969 song "We Can Be Together," which urged the young to band together, tear down the walls of oppression, and forge "a new continent of earth and fire." And it was all driven home by the roaring bass of Jack Casady.

As Casady and Lesh strove for sonic refinement in the United States, another iconoclastic musician was seeking an original approach to the electric bass. Like Lesh, he was classically trained; like Casady, he saw the bass guitar as an equal voice—but this Scottish-born innovator brought a unique vision to his music that challenged just about every established notion of what a bass player should be.

Chapter 12: Jack It Up

Jack Bruce believed the bass guitar was a new instrument that required a new approach. Bruce had been playing jazz on upright when he was introduced to the electric bass, and he had an instant affinity for the smaller instrument: "I fell in love with it," he said in a 1993 interview. "I thought, Wow, this is easy and it's *loud*."

Bruce's precocious musical talent earned him a scholarship to the Royal Academy of Music in Glasgow, Scotland, where he studied cello and composition. He was more interested in bass, though, which he studied independently and played at night in dance bands. But he soon grew discontented, both at the rigid British class system that discriminated against him (he was the son of a factory worker) and at the school's strict regulations. After he was told he could no longer play in dance bands if he wished to remain at the academy, Jack took off for London.

Bruce was at first a "jazz purist" who played only upright and looked askance at the developing rock scene. His outlook began to change after a stint with the English bluesman Alexis Korner, and he took notice of the bass guitar in 1962 after hearing a bassist named Roy Babbington play one. Soon after that, Jack was hired for a session with the Jamaican guitarist Ernest Ranglin—and told to bring along a bass guitar. "So I went to a music shop and borrowed a Guild [Starfire] semi-acoustic bass," recalled Bruce. "It had those nylon tapewound strings that kind of went 'boink.'"

Intrigued by the playability and volume of the bass guitar, Bruce started to listen more closely to recordings that featured it. "I began to hear James Jamerson," he said. "Listening to those Tamla recordings, I began to see the possibilities of the bass guitar. It wasn't limited to playing root notes four to the bar; it could actually be a melody instrument—

which it very much was in the hands of James." Equipped with a Japanese-made Top 20 bass guitar that was "pretty monstrous," Jack started to work out his ideas for the instrument, applying both upright technique and his desire to play melodically.

While Bruce was woodshedding on the electric bass, he was still performing on upright in the Graham Bond Organisation, an R&B/jazz group that included drummer Ginger Baker. In 1965, when guitarist John McLaughlin quit the band, Jack saw an opportunity to apply the bass guitar in a new way. He purchased a Fender Bass VI and began to play it with the group, trying to cover both the guitar and bass functions with his parts.

Bruce deliberately avoided using a Fender Precision Bass or Jazz Bass, despite their market dominance at the time. "They had a wonderful sound," he explained, "but I thought, Well, that's a bit limiting. Even in those days, I was trying to find different sounds and different approaches to the bass guitar." The Bass VI, with its 30" scale, triple-pickup configuration, and tremolo bar, was a long way from a standard Fender bass—and Bruce's experimental parts were a long way from standard bass playing. As can be heard on the Graham Bond album *The Sound of '65*, Jack's lines were creative if not yet fully formed. His "busy" playing eventually bothered Ginger Baker so much that he got Bruce fired from the band.

"I was at a low point," recalled Jack, "and I thought, Well, that's it. I'll probably give it up now and get a job in a factory." And then he got a call from Marvin Gaye, who was in town to do a television show. Gaye hired Bruce for the TV gig and offered him a spot in his road band. Although Jack turned down the touring job, his confidence was restored—and less than a year later he was invited to join a new band called Cream, with guitarist Eric Clapton...and Ginger Baker. (Clapton, not knowing the history between Bruce and Baker, had told Ginger that he thought Jack should be in the band. Baker, at first aghast, eventually agreed.)

The three musicians first got together to play in June 1966, and Bruce immediately knew they were onto something. With Clapton's passionate,

Jack Bruce was one of the few bassists to adopt the Fender Bass VI. Despite its narrow string spacing, he plucked the strings with his fingers. Bruce used the Bass VI for several years in the late '60s and played it on *Fresh Cream.*

blues-tinged guitar on top and Baker's jazz-inflected drumming creating a fluid rhythmic underpinning, Jack's restless bass parts worked perfectly. Still armed with the Bass VI, he began to unfold a style that would reach creative maturity before the trio flew apart little more than two years later.

Jack Bruce has often said it was his goal to play the bass guitar "like a guitar," but it's important to remember that he was a legitimate jazz bassist and a trained composer before he ever touched an electric bass. As enthusiastically as he attacked his new instrument with bends, end-to-end runs, chords, and other guitaristic devices (and few bassists have ever matched Bruce's enthusiasm), he never lost his grounding in the instrument's essential support function. That "crossover" nature of his playing makes it so fascinating—and is one reason it was so influential. For bassists, Bruce's work in Cream was a sign that good bass playing and a high degree of creative freedom were not mutually exclusive. It was a call to liberation.

While Cream was conceived as a trio of equals, Bruce was in many ways its *de facto* leader. Despite a huge following that hailed him as "God," Clapton was a reluctant vocalist and an inexperienced songwriter who would labor for months over a single composition. Baker was an accomplished drummer but hardly suited for the task of fronting the band. That left Jack Bruce to not only play bass but also be the lead vocalist and primary songwriter (along with his partner, lyricist Pete Brown). Because he

was so involved in creating the
group's material, Bruce shaped it to
give himself maximum expression as
a bassist.

On *Fresh Cream*, recorded in the
fall of 1966, Bruce played both the
Fender Bass VI and the upright ("Four
Until Late") as well as singing, playing
harmonica, and writing or co-writing
about half of the material. The crude
production didn't do justice to Jack's
still-emerging sound, but the album's
mixture of blues and pop concepts—
and its hints at wide-open jamming—
made it clear this new band had
tremendous potential.

Just before Cream recorded
Disraeli Gears—which
included their first big hit,
"Sunshine of Your Love"—
Jack Bruce bought a
secondhand Gibson EB-3 in
London. This small, short-
scale bass proved to be the
perfect instrument for
Bruce's exploratory,
"guitar-like" style.

Between the recording of *Fresh Cream* and *Disraeli Gears*, Bruce
stopped using the Bass VI. "The first time we came to the States, that was
the instrument I brought with me," he explained. "It had been severely
painted by some Dutch artists called The Fool. They painted all these psychedelic scenes on Eric's [Gibson SG] guitar and my bass, but unfortunately it was all done the night before we left on tour—and it never dried!
So that was partly the reason for giving up that instrument."

After trying a Danelectro Long Horn Bass for a while, Bruce settled on
the Gibson bass that would be his main instrument for nearly a decade.
"I found a Gibson EB-3 secondhand in a London music shop and immediately liked it a lot. It had an extremely wide neck. I went to the Gibson
factory years later and told them about this instrument, and they said,
'Oh, no, it couldn't be; we never made one like that.' The neck was either
a mistake or something they tried and forgot about. It wasn't the greatest
of instruments, but it was useful at the time."

The Gibson Electric Bass made its debut in 1953. It had a 30¹/₂" scale length—apparently to make it more attractive to guitarists—but was equipped with an extendable endpin for vertical playing, like an upright bass. Only 546 were made before Gibson dropped the model in 1958. It was briefly reintroduced in 1970.

Bright Ideas & Near Misses

These days, well-known musicians routinely endorse instruments in return for getting them for little or nothing, so it's interesting that Jack Bruce went shopping for his own bass—and bought it used. It's also interesting that it was a Gibson bass. Gibson is one of the oldest and most respected names in the guitar business, but the history of their electric basses is largely a saga of missed opportunities.

As we saw in Chapter 2, Lloyd Loar was the first person to think of applying electricity to the problem of getting more volume from a stringed bass instrument. He presented his ideas to Gibson's management in the 1920s, but was turned down. Fifteen years later, someone at the company came even closer to getting a jump on the bass business with the Gibson Electric Bass Guitar of 1938–40. Only two of these instruments were built, however, and Gibson never exploited the idea. It wasn't until after the Fender Precision Bass had appeared on the market that Gibson once again turned its attention to the idea of building an electric bass.

The Gibson Electric Bass was introduced in 1953. It had a shorter scale (30$\frac{1}{2}$") than the Fender Precision, which should have made it even more appealing to guitarists. But its body was violin-shaped, and it came equipped with a telescoping endpin, so it could be played vertically. This would seem to indicate that the target market was upright bassists. The single pickup was placed at the end of the neck (in contrast to the mid-body placement on the Precision Bass), which contributed to the Gibson's deeper but less distinct tone. The tuning machines were mounted banjo-style with rear-facing keys. The overall impression was one of design confusion—just who was supposed to play this instrument?—which might help to explain its limited appeal.

Gibson tried again in 1958 with the EB-2. (The original Electric Bass was renamed the EB-1 but soon dropped from the company's line.) This new model established a practice that would be a predominant theme in Gibson's bass offerings over the years: it was essentially a guitar body with a bass neck attached. The EB-2 was the partner of the ES-335 and shared the guitar's semi-hollow body design. Like the Electric Bass/EB-1, it had a 30$\frac{1}{2}$" scale length and a single pickup mounted at the end of the neck. The tuners were again the banjo-style units, suggesting that Gibson was building its new bass model simply by grafting necks from the Electric Bass/EB-1 onto ES guitar bodies. This may have been efficient for the factory, but it showed that Gibson was not giving much thought to designing bass guitars as unique instruments.

A year after the EB-2 was introduced, Gibson offered the EB-0. (Even though the numeric designation is a zero, but it's usually spoken as the letter "O.") Why the company decided to use a model-numbering

Gibson's second electric bass model, the EB-2, was introduced in 1958. Setting a trend that would define many of the company's bass models over the years, this semi-hollow instrument was the "partner" of a guitar—in this case, the ES-335. The single humbucking pickup was notable for its murky sound.

sequence that went from one to two to zero is anybody's guess. Once again this bass was a "partner" instrument, the guitar in question being the Les Paul Jr. Two years later, its body shape was modified to match the newly introduced SG guitar, and a two-pickup version called the EB-3 was added to the line. Thanks to its use by Jack Bruce in Cream, the EB-3 had a brief period of popularity in the late '60s and early '70s, but it was discontinued in 1979.

Gibson's most successful bass design was probably the Thunderbird, which debuted in 1963. Once again conceived in tandem with a guitar model (the Firebird), the original Thunderbird offered neck-through-body construction and one- and two-pickup configurations. Most important, it had a 34" scale length that matched the Fender basses—and it blasted out a powerful, biting tone that got the attention of top players like John Entwistle. By 1965, though, Gibson had altered the body (going from the so-called "reverse" shape to "non-reverse") and dropped the neck-through-body construction for the more conventional approach of gluing the neck to the body. The Thunderbird, in various flavors, has gone in and out of production ever since, and it is still a favorite with many heavy metal and hard rock bassists.

Bach Meets Rock

Jack Bruce couldn't have cared less about Gibson's problems in the bass market. He found his EB-3 perfectly suitable for Cream, especially since it was easy to play while he was singing. He used it to record *Disraeli Gears* in May 1967, and the change in his sound was quite apparent. With fellow bassist Felix Pappalardi producing and his role as the primary vocalist and songwriter firmly established, Jack was front and center throughout the album that launched Cream to superstardom. His bass playing was strikingly bold: more and more, his parts were functioning as countermelodies to Clapton's guitar lines, and they were filled with string bends, upper-register fills, and other "guitar-like" devices. Bruce's tone had become fat and brash, with the characteristic edge of distortion that would become his trademark.

Beginning with *Disraeli Gears* and carrying through *Wheels of Fire* and *Goodbye* (and the subsequent releases of live material from Cream's 1968 shows), Bruce's bass lines grew increasingly improvisational. Impatient with the conventions of rock and R&B bass playing, Jack simply discarded them for a new approach that owed as much to his study of J.S. Bach and Charles Mingus as it did to any of his electric bass predecessors. Seen from the perspective of 30-plus years, some of it might sound self-indulgent and a bit sloppy, but at the time it was a revelation.

At the beginning of the '60s, the Fender bass had gained only a small degree of acceptance, mostly in the restricted world of studio playing. Thanks to the brilliant and influential ideas of James Jamerson and Paul McCartney, it began to approach its full potential. Musicians such as John Entwistle, Jack Casady, Phil Lesh, and Jack Bruce carried this crusade forward, forging new styles that made the bass an equal voice—and making their groups that much more popular and powerful. The music of the leading rock bands became the soundtrack for the social changes that were driven forward by the generation that came of age in the late '60s. While some of the ideals may seem naïve today, the impact of those turbulent years cannot be denied. The America that emerged in the 1970s after the end of the Vietnam War bore little resemblance to the complacent and conforming U.S.A. of the 1950s. And rock music— fueled by the Fender bass and its descendants—had helped to power the revolution.

Something else was happening in the late '60s, too. The influence of the Fender bass was beginning to reach beyond rock and have an impact on other musical styles. A young bassist in Oakland, California, was one of the key players in this movement, and his far-reaching influence was based on a spur-of-the-moment decision to strike the strings in a different way.

Chapter 13: Thumbslingers

When Leo Fender designed the Precision Bass, he assumed players would pluck the strings with their thumbs; that's why the early P-Basses have a finger rest on the *G*-string side of the body. If you put the fingernails of your right hand against this rest, your thumb will be in position over the strings about midway between the pickup cover and the end of the neck. Striking the strings with a downstroke—assuming the bass is equipped with heavy flatwound strings and its rubber string mute—produces a thick, meaty tone much like that of an upright bass.

Many of the early electric bassists did indeed use this right-hand technique. Fender pioneer Monk Montgomery, although he was accustomed to playing the upright with his fingers, said: "The downstroke came to me naturally, and I would just strike the string that way. I had no examples or influences."

When guitarists such as Carol Kaye and Joe Osborn began to adopt the Fender bass, they held onto their flatpicks. This gave their attack a "click" that was advantageous in the studio, especially since the recording gear of the time did not have the sophisticated equalization that would later help bassists get a good sound regardless of their right-hand technique.

By the early 1960s, many bassists had started to use another right-hand technique: positioning the hand above the strings and using their fingertips to pull the strings. (Noticing this, Fender eventually made the finger rest into a thumb rest by moving it to a position near the lowest string.) This technique was similar to the pizzicato style many jazz bassists use, plucking the strings with one or two right-hand fingers. James Jamerson used only his index finger—which he called "The

Hook"—but most Fender bassists preferred to alternate their index and middle fingers. (Later, some bassists would use three or even four fingers for more speed.) This fingerstyle technique produces a sound that is nearly as thick as a "thumb tone" but without the harshness of a "pick tone." Alternating the fingers allows more rapid playing and aids string muting, because the plucking finger naturally comes to rest against the adjacent string.

Muting, or string damping, is an important and much overlooked aspect of bass technique. With its rubber mute in place, the original P-Bass did not require much damping by the player, because the notes were dead—that is, they did not have much sustain. When bassists began to remove the mute and play with a pick or their fingers, they discovered

Bootsy Collins played one of the funkiest bass lines of all time on James Brown's "Sex Machine" and went on to achieve stardom with Parliament/Funkadelic and as a solo artist. Slapping is just one element of his complex technique, which includes a variety of pats and slides as well as classic fingerstyle playing. Bootsy was also a pioneer in the use of bass effects, getting some truly wild sounds with the help of his Mu-Tron III envelope follower and Big Muff fuzz pedals.

that the strings would sometimes ring longer than they wanted them to, or their hands might brush the strings accidentally. This produced unwanted sounds that often clashed with the note being struck, causing muddy and indistinct tone. (The problem is especially acute with a bright tone. As John Entwistle said, "You can't play sloppily.... I had to clean it up and find a fluid way of damping the notes so they didn't blur into each other.")

To remedy this, bass players learned to mute their strings in different ways, using either their right- or left-hand fingers or the heel of the right hand to damp the strings not being played. Many bassists have developed this technique without thinking about it much—they have simply learned how to position their hands to produce a clean sound. (For guitarists who double on bass, this can be one of the hardest aspects of bass technique. Simply picking up an electric bass and playing it like a guitar, without good string-muting technique, can produce ugly, clattering sounds.) With the introduction of roundwound strings—with their long sustain and bright, ringing tone—string-muting technique became crucial to good bass sound.

Slapping

By the late 1960s, most Fender bassists were using either their fingers or a pick to strike the strings. And then a young musician named Larry Graham had a different idea.

Like many of the great musical innovations, Graham's new bass technique was born of necessity. Larry had grown up in a musical family in Oakland, California, where he learned to play drums, clarinet, and saxophone as well as guitar. By the time he was 15, he was working in a group led by his mother, who sang and played piano. "We had a trio," Graham recalled, "me, my mother, and a drummer. One club we played at had an organ with bass footpedals. I started playing the footpedals while I sang and played the guitar, and it sounded great. Then one night the organ broke down, and we sounded kind of empty without the bottom end. The next day I rented a St. George solid-body bass from a store called Music Unlimited; I planned to play it temporarily until the organ could be fixed. It turned out they couldn't get the necessary parts anymore, so I was stranded on the bass. Meanwhile, thinking that my stint as a bassist would be limited, I plucked the strings with my thumb and never bothered to learn the normal right-hand technique, with two fingers over the top."

Graham faced another crisis when the drummer departed. "That was when I started to thump the strings with my thumb to make up for not having a bass drum. And I also plucked the strings with my index finger to fill in the snare backbeat. Over time, I got it down pretty good, but I wasn't thinking in terms of creating anything new; I was just trying to do my job—to provide as much of a foundation as I could."

As it turned out, Graham had invented a new way of playing bass that would be instrumental in launching a style of music called funk. Instead of using his thumb for downstrokes, he was "thumping"—hammering the strings with the side of his thumb near the base of the neck, which bounced the strings off the frets and produced a tone that was both deep and clear. (The sound is

Larry Graham invented his "thumping and plucking" technique to compensate for the lack of a drummer on club dates. It proved to be highly influential on other bassists and was a key element in the development of funk. Larry used a mid-'60s Jazz Bass he called "Sunshine" in Sly & the Family Stone and later in his own band, Graham Central Station. (Sly Stone himself contributed some cool bass playing after Graham left the band, especially on the 1973 album *Fresh*.)

Louis Johnson of the Brothers Johnson played devastating slap bass on such '70s funk hits as "I'll Be Good to You" and "Strawberry Letter 23." Johnson has called slapping "a matter of natural evolution for me," noting that he developed the technique before he heard Larry Graham.

much like that of a bass drum and a plucked bass note played in unison, which was what Graham was trying to imitate.) To this, he added a second technique: pulling out the *G* string and letting it snap back against the neck, producing a short, percussive note. Larry calls this "plucking," but it is usually referred to as "popping." The combination of both techniques is now generally called "slapping and popping" or simply "slapping," and it has been widely adopted by electric bassists in many styles.

Larry Graham's new style came to the attention of a wide audience after he joined Sly & the Family Stone and played on such hit albums as *Dance to the Music* (1968) and *Stand!* (1969). These recordings are important not only because of Graham's bass innovations but because of their social impact. Sly Stone's band was unique, even in the "peace and love" environment of the late '60s: it brought together male and female musicians of different races and ethnic backgrounds to play music that blended elements of R&B and rock in songs that often had strong social and political messages. Once again, the Fender bass was playing a prominent role in driving home music that was intended to be a force for positive change. (Little did Sly suspect that "Everyday People" would later become the theme for a series of Toyota commercials.)

Funk Meets Jazz

By the early 1970s, Larry Graham's "thumping and plucking" style was showing up in the work of other influential funk bass players like Bootsy

There's more to funk than slapping. Francis Rocco Prestia of Tower Of Power set the standard for fingerstyle funkiness with his churning 16th-note line on "What Is Hip?" (*Tower of Power*, 1973), which "changed the course of history," according to Will Lee. Prestia used Precision Basses for many years.

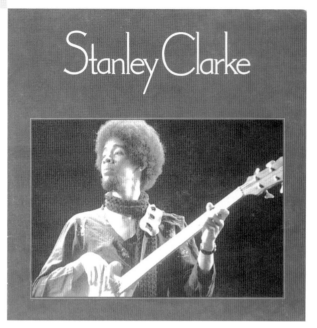

Trained as a classical musician, Stanley Clarke emerged as the first great jazz-rock electric bassist. His amazing technical facility and bright, percussive sound with *Return To Forever* and on his 1974 solo album dazzled listeners and set a new standard for bass players. Clarke is known for using a wide array of Alembic basses, in standard, tenor, and piccolo tunings.

Collins and Louis Johnson (who has said he developed the idea independently, before hearing Graham). It also caught the ear of Stanley Clarke.

Clarke was a formally trained bassist who had attended the Philadelphia Academy of Music, but he also listened to and performed both jazz and rock. Although the upright was his main instrument, he had been playing the electric bass since the age of 16—and he was very skillful on both instruments. Clarke's early professional work included jazz gigs and commercial sessions in New York City, where word of his talent quickly spread. In 1971, he was invited to join Return To Forever, a seminal jazz-rock band led by keyboardist Chick Corea.

The drummer in Corea's group was Lenny White, who showed Larry Graham's new bass technique to Clarke. "Lenny didn't really know what he was doing on bass," recalled Stanley, "but he had great rhythm. Since I learned from him, my slapping was a little different." Clarke soon became renowned for his ability to apply the new technique to complex jazz compositions. "Chick wrote tunes in $A\flat$, $C\sharp$, everything. I didn't get a chance to slap in E until I did my solo stuff, and that was like a release—*whew!*—because it was so much easier."

Clarke had been using a Gibson EB-2 when he joined Return To Forever, but in 1973 he found out about a new kind of bass guitar that was better suited to his needs. "We were playing at a club in San Francisco, and this guy came up to me and said my playing was great but my sound was atrocious. It was Rick Turner, who was with Alembic. He had a bass with him, so I tried it out. It was like a new bass player was born that night—suddenly, I could play anything I heard in my head." Clarke has been closely identified with Alembic ever since, and his large collection of Alembic basses eventually included piccolo basses (tuned *EADG* an octave higher, like the bottom four strings of a guitar), tenor basses (tuned *ADGC* or *AEBF*♯), and other specialized instruments.

In 1972, Clarke recorded a largely overlooked solo album, *Children of Forever*, on which he played only the upright. But his 1974 eponymous solo release on Nemperor Records (later reissued on an Epic CD) astounded listeners—and sent bass players scrambling to the woodshed. The cover showed a confident Stanley, Alembic bass in hand, ready to take on the world. The album's first four tunes were a

Five years after Leo Fender sold his company to CBS, he started a new company, Music Man, with Forrest White and Tom Walker. White came up with the idea of a 3+1 headstock, and Leo did the rest, designing a great-sounding single-pickup bass that represented another step in the evolutionary process he had begun with the Precision Bass.

stunning showcase of his electric bass technique. There had never been a bass sound quite like that, nor had anyone ever heard such a dazzling array of runs, slaps, strums, pops, chords, and assorted other techniques, all delivered at lightning speed and with crisp, clear articulation.

School Days followed two years later, and by then Clarke had firmly established himself as the first jazz-rock bass virtuoso. It seemed unimaginable that another musician could play the electric bass with such a distinctive, personal sound and astounding technique—but no sooner had Stanley Clarke demonstrated his greatness than another brash young musician came along, Fender Jazz Bass in hand, proclaiming himself the greatest.

Verdine White of Earth, Wind & Fire was another great fingerstyle funk bassist. His work was distinguished by fluid melodies and sophisticated harmonic ideas that reflected his background in jazz and classical music as well as classic R&B. He played Fender Telecaster, Precision, and Jazz basses on such enduring EW&F hits as "Shining Star," "Singasong," and "Can't Hide Love."

Chapter 14: The World's Greatest Bass Player

Clarence Leo Fender and John Francis Pastorius III made an odd creative partnership. By all accounts, Leo was a shy, diffident man who loved nothing better than tinkering in his lab. He shunned attention and was sensitive about his lack of a college degree. He never learned to play the instruments he spent his life designing and building. Jaco was loud and brash and outrageous. He craved attention and dressed oddly. Even as a child, he was always eager to perform for an audience and proclaim himself the best at whatever he did. And after he gave up the drums and picked up a Fender Jazz Bass, it wasn't long before he had crowned himself the World's Greatest Bass Player. It was an incredible boast—and it was true.

Jaco was a pure electric bassist. He never played the guitar. He fooled around on upright bass occasionally, but pronounced the big instrument "a pain in the ass…too much work for too little sound." He probably would have followed in his father's footsteps and become a drummer, but after he broke his wrist playing football he found it difficult to hit the snare drum properly. At the age of 15, he picked up an electric bass to sub for another local player. He took to the instrument quickly, and according to his brother Rory had become "the best bass player in the entire state [of Florida]" by the time he was 18.

Although Jaco's first Jazz Bass was supposedly a '60 model he got from a friend, this snapshot shows a teenage Jaco with a new instrument with block fingerboard inlays, which indicate it was probably made in late 1966 or early 1967.

After starting out on a pawnshop instrument, Jaco acquired a Fender Jazz Bass. According to a number of sources, this was a used '60 J-Bass he got from his friend and fellow bassist Bob Bobbing. Bill Milkowski quotes Jaco as saying he replaced the "stack knob" controls on this bass with the

Jaco's first steady gig was with a local band called Las Olas Brass. This show was at Teen Town, which Jaco said was "a place I used to go dance when I was 13." It later inspired one of his compositions for Weather Report.

three-knob setup found on later Jazz Basses because the bass "just didn't seem to have enough punch" with the original wiring.

This is an interesting story, although there are photographs of Jaco that tell a slightly different tale. One of these appeared in the September '97 issue of *Bass Player* with the caption "Future Jazz Great: The day Jaco got his first J-Bass, in Oakland Park, Florida." In this color snapshot, a teenage Jaco is shown standing in the yard of a typical South Florida home, proudly holding what appears to be a brand-new sunburst Jazz Bass, complete with the chrome covers over the pickup and bridge. The fingerboard has mother-of-pearl block inlays rather than dots, indicating the bass was not made before late 1966. On the next page, there is a black & white photo of Jaco onstage with the Las Olas Brass, "circa 1967," playing what looks like the same bass.

There are numerous photos of Jaco later in his career playing a fretted Jazz Bass that is an early model with dot markers on the fingerboard, and it has the three-knob controls. So it appears likely that he may, indeed, have owned a '60 J-Bass that he modified with the later wiring. Jaco was a notorious storyteller, and he told various versions of incidents in his life in different interviews. Sensing, no doubt, that a used, pre-CBS Jazz Bass was a "cooler" instrument than a brand-new bass made after 1965, he probably rearranged the details of his bass

One of Jaco's main basses was a fretted '60 Jazz Bass. He modified it by installing the three-knob controls found in later J-Basses because he felt this gave the bass more punch at louder volumes

acquisitions. Ultimately, though, it doesn't really matter when his basses were made or from whom he got them.

At some point Jaco got another Jazz Bass. This instrument, reportedly a '62, was to become the "Bass of Doom," which he used to record much of his most famous music. In an act that probably would have horrified Leo Fender, Jaco yanked out the frets and filled the slots with wood putty. (He gave varying accounts of how this was done: pulling them out with a pair of pliers, prying them out with a butter knife.) To protect the fingerboard from the abrasion of Rotosound roundwound strings, Jaco coated the wood with several layers of marine epoxy. This produced a smooth, hard surface that gave the bass a unique "singing" quality.

"I have a fretless bass, so it's virtually like I'm playing a wood bass," Jaco said. "In other words, the strings go into the wood on the neck, but being that it's a bass guitar, it gets that bright sound and direct sound. It's

Jaco got his distinctive sound from a '62 Jazz Bass that he had defretted. He coated the fingerboard with marine epoxy, which created a hard surface that stood up well to round-wound strings. His favorite amp was the Acoustic 360, and he sometimes used an MXR Digital Delay.

just legitimate vibrato. That's it—there are no tricks. It's all in the hands. It's like I'm the first guy to be using a fretless and really get down and play it. Because nobody can play it—they cannot play it in tune. I play in tune like a cello player."

Imprecision Bass

Jaco was not the first musician to use a fretless electric bass—that honor may go to Bill Wyman, of all people—but he was correct in his assessment that he was the first to really "get down and play it" consistently and with good intonation. Before Jaco, the fretless was little more than a footnote in the story of the electric bass; after Jaco, it became an entire chapter.

The first production fret-less bass was the Ampeg AUB-1, introduced in 1966. It had a scroll peghead, an extra-long 34$^1/2$" scale length, and a diaphragm pickup mounted under the bridge.

Rick Danko used a
Precision Bass on many of
The Band's classic
recordings. He later
adopted an Ampeg fretless
that was modified with
Fender pickups.

Bill Wyman became a fretless pioneer more or less by accident. Originally a guitarist, he had purchased his first bass guitar in 1961 after being "staggered by [the] impact" of the sound of an electric bass in a local band. Wyman's first bass was an inexpensive Japanese instrument, which he immediately modified by reshaping the body and pulling out all the frets. He had intended to refret it, but found he could play it quite well by carefully placing his fingers on the fret slots. The impromptu fretless remained a favored instrument for years (Wyman has praised its "pure and deep and rich" sound), and it can be heard on many Rolling Stones recordings—most notably, "Paint It Black."

The first production fretless was the Ampeg AUB-1 "horizontal bass," which debuted in 1966. The instrument was aimed at upright players; it had a scroll headstock, an "extra long" scale length of 34$\frac{1}{2}$", and a weirdly shaped body with two *f*-holes that went entirely through it. Thanks to its unusual bridge-mounted diaphragm pickup, it could use gut strings to better simulate acoustic-bass sound (at least in theory). The AUB-1 and its fretted partner, the AEB-1, didn't put a noticeable dent in Fender bass sales, although a few players found them interesting. One was Rick Danko of The Band, who used an Ampeg fretless during the recording of *Cahoots* and *Rock of Ages*.

Fender first offered a fretless Precision Bass in 1970. There's a certain degree of irony to this, given that the Precision name was derived from the instrument's fretted fingerboard. (Forrest White reported: "I asked Leo how he came up with the name Precision Bass. He said, 'It was simple. If a player noted the right fret, the tone was right on—a precision result.'") The fretless P-Bass sold modestly; early owners included Freebo, who did some nice work with one on several early Bonnie Raitt albums, and Sting of the Police.

It apparently never occurred to Fender to offer a fretless Jazz Bass, even at the height of Jaco's popularity. This was a sign of how out of touch the company had become by the mid '70s. Not only had quality control slipped, but the important advisory role musicians played in the pre-CBS era had largely vanished. Product decisions were based on the bottom line, not the music scene. Fortunately, this trend was reversed in the 1980s, when a group of Fender executives led by Bill Schultz purchased the company and took important steps to restore product quality and responsiveness to artists. So it's not surprising the company's line in recent years has included several fretless Jazz Basses, one of which is a special "Jaco Pastorius Relic Jazz Bass" made by the Fender Custom Shop.

Triumph & Tragedy

The fretless Jazz Bass, strung with Rotosound strings and plugged into an Acoustic 360 amp, was the tool Jaco needed to realize his creative vision. Many of his early gigs were with R&B bands, where he perfected a percolating 16th-note style—influenced by a South Florida bassist named Carlos Garcia and studio ace Jerry Jemmott—that gave the music incredible forward motion. Jaco mastered the technique of playing harmonics, using both natural harmonics (which are played by placing a finger lightly on the string without depressing it) and artificial harmonics (which involve using an extended finger like a capo and picking behind it). This gave Jaco a tremendously extended range to work with, transcending the supposed limitations of the bass. He got the most from the expressive capabilities of the fretless fingerboard, creating long, fluid

One of the finest of Jaco's disciples, British bassist Pino Palladino has a distinctive style that has enhanced many hits, including Paul Young's "Wherever I Lay My Hat (That's My Home)" and Don Henley's "Sunset Grill." His favorite fretless is a '79 Music Man StingRay.

Fender offered a fretless version of the Precision Bass in 1970, thereby defying the instrument's name, which was based on the precise intonation the frets offered. Despite the incredible impact of Jaco Pastorius, Fender did not offer a fretless Jazz Bass until many years later.

melodic lines filled with slides and expressive vibrato. He found the most effective double-stops and used them to fill out his parts. Taking a cue from Jimi Hendrix, he created a flamboyant stage presence that included cross-stage slides and spectacular flips. And, perhaps because of his training as a drummer, Jaco played everything with uncanny rhythmic accuracy.

In 1975, Jaco auditioned—solo—for Bobby Colomby, who was the drummer with Blood, Sweat & Tears and had a production deal with Epic Records. Colomby described the event to Bill Milkowski: "So Jaco plugs in his bass and starts playing. As I sat there listening, my eyes started bugging out and my hair was standing on end. I couldn't believe it. He wasn't kidding—he *was* the greatest bass player in the world! I had heard hundreds of bassists in my time, but none of them even approached the facility that Jaco showed that afternoon. I was absolutely stunned by what he was doing on the bass. He was definitely coming out of the James Jamerson and Jerry Jemmott style of playing, but he went well beyond their scope. He was doing things on the bass that I had never heard anybody do before—harmonics, chording, impossibly fast lines…. He was truly a phenomenon."

Thanks to Colomby's enthusiastic endorsement, Jaco got a solo deal with Epic. The LP that resulted, titled simply *Jaco Pastorius*, was recorded in late 1975 and released in 1976. It is the single most important and influential solo recording ever made by an electric bassist. It shattered any notions that the Fender bass was an instrument of limited expression. It proved that a bass player could function effectively as the lead voice and the foundation—and do them both at the same time. It sent an entire generation of bassists scurrying to their practice rooms. (Dave LaRue said, "I was at Berklee when Jaco's first solo album came out. Everybody in the bass department threw up their hands and said, 'Okay, let's start over.'") Most of all, *Jaco Pastorius*—released 25 years after Leo Fender had introduced his new instrument—proved the Fender bass had truly come of age.

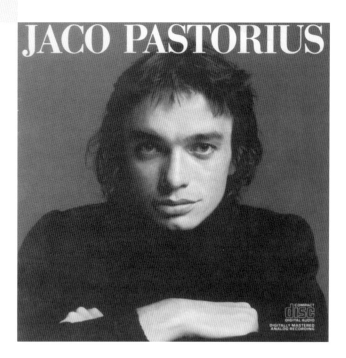

The release of Jaco's first solo album in 1976 was a watershed event in the history of the electric bass guitar. On such brilliant tunes as "Donna Lee," "Continuum," "Portrait of Tracy," and "Come On, Come Over," Jaco demonstrated the full expressive potential of his instrument. In the liner notes of a CD reissue in 2000, Pat Metheny wrote: "That this is the most auspicious debut album of the past quarter-century is inarguable. As with all great recordings, the force of its value becomes more evident as time passes."

Jaco's career took off after his solo album was recorded. He played with Pat Metheny on the guitarist's stunning debut, *Bright Size Life*. He was invited to join Weather Report and immediately made a strong contribution to the album *Black Market*. He went on to spark some of the group's finest work on such recordings as *Heavy Weather, Mr. Gone, Night Passage*, and the potent live album *8:30*, which showcased his solo feature, "Slang." From 1976 to 1980, not only did Jaco light a fire under Weather Report with his playing, he contributed a number of evocative and well-crafted compositions to their repertoire, such as "Havona," "Teen Town," and "Three Views of a Secret." During this period, he was also a guest star on a number of records. He collaborated with Joni Mitchell on four albums, including *Hejira*, which has some of his freshest and most lyrical playing. Jaco went on the road with Mitchell's all-star band in 1979 and is a powerful presence on the *Shadows and Light* album and video recorded during the tour.

And then, like a meteor, Jaco tumbled from the heavens. Overwhelmed by fame and suffering from a mental disorder exacerbated by drug and alcohol abuse, he fell apart. The years from 1980 until his death in 1987 were marked by a great deal of turmoil and very little good music.

Despite his tragic decline, Jaco Pastorius forever changed the way the Fender bass was played and perceived. David Hungate summed it up in a *Bass Player* interview: "You have to separate electric bass playing into two periods: Before Jaco and After Jaco. Most of us who thought we had our acts together in the early '70s were faced with a serious decision the first time we heard him: give up the instrument or try to figure out what the hell he was doing. I don't believe any other individual has so totally revolutionized and expanded the approach to an instrument."

As the first generation of post-Jaco bassists began to emerge in the 1980s, many musicians struggled to get beyond mere imitation. The "Jaco clones" were everywhere. But there were a few individuals who had quite different ideas about bass playing. One was a New York studio bassist who had been trying for several years to make a fundamental change to the instrument itself—and whose advocacy of the 6-string bass altered the course of the instrument's development.

Chapter 15: Battleships & B Strings

A hybrid with a Precision neck on a Jazz body, Anthony Jackson's "Career Girl" Fender bass was his main studio instrument in the early 1970s. In this photo, it's on the right, resting against Jackson's left knee. Jackson ordered his first contrabass guitar from Carl Thompson in 1975. He's holding it up with his right hand—notice the tight string spacing compared to the Fender. The other two instruments are Fodera/Jackson 6-strings made in 1988 (lower left) and 1989 (in Jackson's lap).

In 1975, as Jaco prepared for his breakthrough debut album, a luthier named Carl Thompson was building an unusual instrument called a "contrabass guitar." Session bassist Anthony Jackson had ordered the new instrument, which had six strings rather than four. One of the extra strings was tuned to *B*, a fourth below a 4-string's open *E*; the other was *C*, a fourth above open *G*.

Jackson had begun to play bass in 1965 at the age of 13, and by 1970 he was already getting studio work. He backed singer Billy Paul on the hit "Me

and Mrs. Jones" and shortly afterward received a writer's credit for his bass line on the O'Jay's "For the Love of Money." Jackson created that unforgettable (and much imitated) part using his newly purchased Maestro phase-shifter pedal and a Fender Precision Bass, which he played with a pick.

As satisfying as that was, Jackson still envisioned sounds he couldn't play on his Fender. The idea for an extended-range instrument kept coming back to him, inspired at least in part by his practice sessions with records by jazz organist Jimmy Smith. While listening to a bass line Smith played on his footpedals, Jackson heard a note that was below the range of his P-Bass; that note was, he later explained, "one I simply had to play."

At first Jackson tried to go lower simply by detuning his bass. While this worked reasonably well if he dropped down only a half- or whole-step,

In 1976, Jimmy Johnson was the first bassist to play a 5-string electric bass tuned *BEADG*. Alembic built the instrument. Johnson soon discovered that the *B* string could produce unwanted noise that cluttered his sound, so he developed a right-hand muting technique based on placing his thumb between the *B* and *E* strings.

larger intervals were a problem. "A little common sense, combined with a willingness to experiment, led me to modify my Fender accordingly," Jackson told Chris Jisi. "I raised the nut, readjusted the truss rod, and did much bridge-fiddling until the instrument felt manageable when tuned down two whole-steps."

Jackson played sessions with his Fender bass tuned this way, including the ones that produced the memorable Chaka Khan albums *Naughty* (1979) and *What Cha' Gonna Do For Me* (1980). As good as they were, the results further convinced Anthony that he needed an all-new instrument. Although he was primarily interested in extending the range of his bass downward, he never considered the idea of adding just one string: "As the lowest-pitched member of the guitar family, the instrument should have had six strings from the beginning. The only reason it had four was because Leo Fender was thinking in application terms of an upright bass, but he built it along guitar lines because that was his training."

When Jackson approached him about building a contrabass guitar, Carl Thompson's reaction was: "Crazy guy! Six strings, low *B*—what are you talkin' about?" But he built one anyway. The first instrument was delivered to Jackson early in 1975. It had a 34" scale length, like a Fender bass, and it worked reasonably well, although Jackson disliked its tight string spacing. After Thompson made one more experimental contrabass—this time with a 44" scale length that was "impractical to finger"—Jackson set out to find another builder who would construct a 6-string bass with wider string spacing. "It's solely to duplicate the string spacing on my Fender 4-string," he explained, "which I've owned since 1972 and feel very comfortable with." The comfortable instrument was a Fender hybrid Jackson had put together from a Precision neck and a Jazz body. Because he had used it on so many successful sessions, he dubbed it "Career Girl."

Ken Smith was the next builder to tackle Jackson's project. He constructed two 6-strings, both with 34" scale lengths. The first instrument was completed in 1981, and Jackson used it for three years even though he felt the string spacing was, once again, too tight. Smith's second instrument arrived in 1984, and Jackson finally approved of the spacing, which matched that of "Career Girl." While its wide neck looked unwieldy—skeptics tended to use nautical terms like "battleship" and "aircraft carrier"—Jackson demonstrated that it could be played with highly musical results. He continued his experiments with instruments made in the shop of Vinnie Fodera, who had been an assistant to Ken Smith. The first Fodera/Jackson contrabass, with a 36" scale length, was built in 1986. More versions have followed (as of this writing, Anthony is using his ninth Fodera instrument), and most of the 6-string basses currently available feature the wide string spacing Jackson had advocated from the beginning.

While Anthony Jackson believed that a contrabass with six strings made the most sense, others thought that five strings might be enough. Jimmy Johnson was probably the first bassist to use a bass with just the additional low *B* string, which was inspired by the *C*-extension upright his father played: "The idea came from my dad, because [some] orchestral basses have extensions that let you go down to low *C*. They have a machine just for that, and I started talking to my dad about how I could do this on electric bass."

Johnson reportedly considered making a device that would work like the *C*-extension of an upright, but abandoned the idea when a string manufacturer told him it would be too much trouble to make an extra-long *E* string. (Phil Kubicki revived this concept in the 1980s; see Chapter 18.) Johnson then settled on the idea of adding a *B* string. He knew that Alembic had built custom 5-string basses with a high *C*, so he ordered one. After it arrived, he modified the nut and bridge to accept the largest-diameter string he could find (.120), which he tuned to *B*—and in 1976 the 5-string bass tuned *BEADG* was born.

Once again, string spacing was an issue. Johnson's first Alembic 5-string, and most of the other early 5's that followed it, had relatively tight spacing. This made it hard for Fender players to adapt; luthiers took notice, and the spacing has slowly been moved out over the years. On a Precision Bass, the string spacing at the bridge (measured from the center of a string to the center of the adjacent one) is $3/4$"; on most contemporary 5-strings, the spacing is $5/8$" to $3/4$".

Leo Fender may have set the standard for string spacing, but the company that bears his name was late to jump into the 5-string market (not counting the Bass V, which had a high *C* string). In the meantime, builders like Roger Sadowsky were more than happy to fill the gap with high-quality, Fender-inspired 5's.

The first graphite neck was a component of an Alembic bass built in 1977. The neck was made by Modulus Graphite, a company founded by San Francisco bassist and aerospace engineer Geoff Gould.

Enter Graphite

The addition of one or two strings—especially the heavy-gauge *B* string, which can be as big as .142 (compared to a .105 *E* string)—puts more strain on a bass neck. This presented a problem to bass builders, many of whom began to look for materials that would help them make stronger necks. One material that looked promising was a high-tech composite of carbon fiber and epoxy resin, commonly (if inaccurately) referred to as "graphite."

The idea of using graphite to make a bass neck came from the fertile mind of Geoff Gould, a bassist who happened to be a satellite engineer at Ford Aerospace in the late 1970s. "I was at a Grateful Dead concert at [San Francisco's] Winterland in October 1974," recalled Gould, "and I noticed that Phil Lesh had this thick lamb's-wool strap to hold his bass. I assumed the bass was really heavy. I was working on the Voyager project at the time, and many of the parts we were using were made from composites, to save weight. It just seemed to me that you ought to be able to do the same thing with a bass."

Gould got in touch with Ron Armstrong and Rick Turner of Alembic, and he showed them samples of the carbon composite used on the space probe. After some consideration, the "war council" at Alembic decided they would collaborate with Gould to build a bass with a graphite neck. Following a period of trial and error, they completed a prototype in the spring of 1976. "We were able to get Stanley Clarke to try it out during the soundcheck before a Return To Forever concert," said Gould. "It was an ideal situation,

This is one of the earliest Modulus Graphite basses, a 6-string built in late '81 or early '82, according to Geoff Gould. It has a quilted-maple top and back and a through-body graphite neck. It was the first Modulus bass made with a 35" scale length—the extra inch is generally considered to improve the sound of the *B* string, and many 5- and 6-string basses are now built with a 35" scale. After seeing a photo of this bass in *Guitar Player*, Phil Lesh contacted Modulus and ordered a 6-string.

because Stanley was using an Alembic bass that was virtually the same in every respect except the neck. The difference in sound was striking."

Alembic built a short-scale bass with a graphite neck and presented it at the January 1977 NAMM trade show, the annual gathering of musical instrument manufacturers, store owners, journalists, and various hangers-on. There was considerable skepticism but also considerable interest, from both bassists and the R&D department of one major manufacturer. (After some preliminary meetings, the company decided against adopting the new technology.) John McVie of Fleetwood Mac purchased the Alembic show bass, and word soon began to spread about this new material.

Rick Turner obtained a design patent, which was assigned to Gould's new business, Modulus Graphite. Alembic was Gould's only customer at first, and a handful of Alembic/Modulus basses were made in 1977–78. Over the next few years, Gould began to produce Fender replacement necks and to build graphite necks for several customers, as well as offering his own basses under the Modulus Graphite name. Furniture-designer-turned-luthier Ned Steinberger took the composite idea to the extreme, introducing a headless, rectangular-bodied, all-graphite bass in 1979. Bassists like Tony Levin, Geddy Lee, and Sting latched onto them, but the fad proved short-lived. Steinberger eventually sold his company to Gibson and in recent years has focused on upright electric basses that meld wood and composites.

Graphite can be used in a less radical way, as a reinforcing material that improves the strength and sound of a conventional wooden instrument. In recent years, builders have used graphite bars to stiffen the necks on many basses, including several Fender models, and combinations of composites with traditional materials are becoming more and more common.

The emerging bass technology of the 1970s was a rite of passage for the instrument. As Alembic's influence spread, more high-end instruments appeared, and the advent of 5- and 6-string basses meant bassists had more choices than ever. What had been a nearly linear development

Ned Steinberger's all-graphite instrument, introduced in 1979, was the most radical departure to date from the original Fender bass design. Tony Levin got the first Steinberger L-series bass, a fretless 4-string. "That instrument had a lot of hardened steel in it, mixed with the graphite," explained Ned Steinberger. "The thing weighed a ton, but that super-stiff, super-heavy construction gave it a really sweet, dynamic sound."

path since the introduction of the Precision Bass began to branch in many directions.

Appropriately, this took place during a time of transition in American society. After the end of U.S. involvement in Vietnam in 1973, the country turned inward. The social unrest of the '60s was replaced by a focus on fashion (most of it bad) and self-involvement. Richard Nixon was brought low by Watergate; Bruce Springsteen hit his creative stride on *Born to Run* (with Gary Tallent pounding away on a Danelectro bass); the startling special effects in *Star Wars* amazed moviegoers; and a new musical genre was in ascendance. The good news: in this style, the bass line often had unusual prominence. The bad news: it was…disco.

Chapter 16: Dance, Dance, Dance

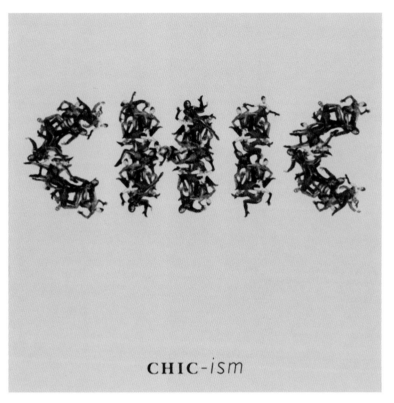

CHIC-ism

The great bass playing of Bernard Edwards was like an oasis in the desert of disco. His playing on Chic's early '70s hits—especially "Good Times"—continues to be recycled by samplers and sequencers. The band made a strong comeback in 1992 on *Chic-ism*, four years before Edwards's untimely death at the age of 43.

In the post-Vietnam era, dancing replaced demonstrations. Popular music remained an important social force, and the charts were filled with songs that combined elements of rock and soul over a relentless (and often stupefying) beat. The new style was called disco.

"Disco was the most self-contained genre in the history of pop, the most clearly defined, and the most despised," wrote Ken Tucker in *Rock of Ages*. "No other pop musical form has ever attracted such rabid partisans and fanatical foes, dividing audiences along racial and sexual lines, even as its function, paradoxically—as music designed to make you dance, dance, dance—was to turn the pop audience into one big happy family."

If disco had a redeeming quality, it was its strong emphasis on rhythm. Many of the most popular disco songs were little more than arranged bass lines, and the best of these came from Chic, who had huge hits with "Le Freak" and "Good Times" in the late 1970s. Chic was led by guitarist Nile Rodgers and bassist Bernard Edwards, who got a thick but well-defined sound from his Music Man StingRay and Ampeg amps. "I love the fat, smooth sound of Jamerson," Edwards explained to Don Snowden, "but I also like to hear the notes I'm playing and the little things that go between the chords, so I always have a lot of top on there." Despite the glitzy disco trappings that surrounded his parts, Edwards worked like a classic R&B bassist, pumping out insistent patterns low on the bass—"I play a lot on the *E* and *A* strings, and I stay down at the first five frets for a fat, chunky sound"—and always focusing on the groove. Chic's sound was highly influential. "Good Times," with its incredibly infectious bass line, has been much copied and sampled, providing the basis for both Queen's "Another One Bites the Dust" and the Sugar Hill Gang's "Rapper's Delight."

Sid Vicious of the Sex Pistols was the quintessential punk bassist. He was angry and nasty, he couldn't really play—and he used a Precision Bass.

The slick superficiality of disco inspired many reactions. One of the most important (and certainly the loudest) of the anti-disco styles was punk rock. Punk bands returned to the essential elements of rock & roll—three-chord songs, cranked-up amps, blistering tempos—and topped it all off with a healthy dose of anger. The bass playing was crude, and the instrument of choice was almost always a black or white Fender Precision, which reflected the genre's emphasis on the basics. Usually slung down around the bassist's knees and attacked with a flatpick, the punk P-Bass was as essential to the music's effect as screaming vocals and an attitude of sneering indifference to the audience.

The quintessential punk bassist—sadly—was probably Sid Vicious of the Sex Pistols. When the band was formed in 1975 ("manufactured" might be a better word, since it was the creation of promoter Malcolm McLaren), Glen Matlock was the bass player. Matlock had some experience as a rock musician, and he brought a reasonable degree of competence to

Aston "Family Man" Barrett and his brother, drummer Carlton Barrett, were the rhythm section for the Wailers. Their seamless grooves set the standard for the reggae rhythm sections that followed.

rabble-rousers like "Anarchy in the U.K." When Matlock quit (or was fired; accounts vary), he was replaced by Vicious, who had no idea how to play bass but was seething with anger at just about everyone and everything. His brutal bass-bashing ensured that the music would remain appropriately anti-technical. Vicious capped off his short career by murdering his girl-friend and then killing himself with a drug overdose. While there were other punk bassists who made stronger musical contributions—Dee Dee Ramone of the Ramones and Paul Simonon of the Clash, for instance—Vicious typified the angry ethos of the punk rocker.

A more sophisticated alternative to disco came from Jamaica. For those who longed for the everybody-get-together days of the late '60s, reggae offered a common bond and inspiring (if sometimes mysterious) messages. Influenced by both calypso and American R&B, reggae had developed into a well-defined style by the early '70s, and its popularity surged after the Wailers released *Burnin'* in 1973. Reggae's unusual start-and-stop bass patterns gave the music much of its hypnotic power. Aston "Family Man" Barrett of the Wailers was one of the founding fathers of the style; armed with a Fender Jazz Bass, he had a huge, deep sound, and his sinuous lines were copied by many other reggae bassists.

Robbie Shakespeare was one of Barrett's most ardent disciples. Origi-nally a guitarist, Shakespeare decided to switch to Fender bass after seeing Family Man perform. "I went to that person and said, 'You have to teach

Robbie Shakespeare and drummer Sly Dunbar—the Riddim Twins—are the greatest rhythm section in reggae history. They have teamed up on an incredible number of recordings, working with everyone from Peter Tosh to Bob Dylan. Shakespeare used a Jazz Bass on many of his classic recordings.

me how to play this thing,'" Shakespeare recalled. "About two days later, he came by my house to show me some things. I said, 'The bass is the instrument for me,' because bass guitar is what makes the song." Shakespeare went on to become one of the most-recorded bassists of his generation, contributing not only to dozens of essential reggae tracks but albums by such high-profile American artists as Grace Jones, Carly Simon, and Bob Dylan. He began his career playing a Fender Jazz Bass and used a number of different instruments over the years, including a Hofner and a Steinberger, before settling on a Paul Reed Smith bass. He explained the choice to Don Snowden: "I like a bass that sounds like a *bass*, deep but clean, have a lot of balls in it. I can get a Fender Jazz sound, a Fender Precision sound, just by turning a knob." Unfortunately, Shakespeare's favorite PRS bass was a discontinued model, although the company got back in the bass business in 2000.

Robbie Shakespeare is an eloquent spokesman for the primacy of bass. "I'm going to make my instrument be the lead, playing the melody. At the same time, it's supposed to interact with the drummer, the guitarist, the keyboards, and the singer, and leave enough space for percussion. If you feel like dubbing on a hundred keyboards, guitars, or vocals, it must not clash. If you take away all the instruments and the bass alone is there, it's supposed to still sound commanding and carry a song."

Hybrids

The most profound musical developments of the 1970s occurred in what might be called "hybrid" styles: crosses between genres that produced music greater than the sum of its parts. In all of these, the Fender bass was a crucial catalyst.

In pop music, the most interesting hybrid group was the Police. Formed in 1977, the band combined the energy of punk rock with the sophistication of reggae. (While some might question their punk credentials—especially since guitarist Andy Summers had already been working as a studio musician—their first single, "Roxanne," was deemed sufficiently upsetting to be banned by the BBC.) The central figure of the band was an English bassist-singer-songwriter named Gordon Sumner, but better known as Sting. Originally a guitarist, he had picked up the bass when his observation of Paul McCartney and Jack Bruce led him to conclude that it would be easier to sing while playing bass. Like McCartney, he quickly learned that being the bassist gave him a great deal of control over the music, especially on reggae-influenced grooves. "In reggae

Sting's playing with the Police combined the frenzy of punk with the melodic sophistication of reggae. In recent years, his favorite bass has been a battered '54 Precision. Because of its delicate condition, the Fender Custom Shop built him an "aged" replica that duplicates the look and sound of the old P-Bass.

there's a power shift toward the bass and away from the guitar," Sting explained to Karl Coryat, "which was very attractive to me as a bassist. The way bass is used in reggae, and particularly dub [which features deep, nearly subsonic bass], is very radical. It's a revolutionary way of loading the rhythm of a bar, and it isn't easy to do."

Berry Oakley was noted for his fluid, melodic style with the Allman Brothers Band. He can be heard at his best on the great 1971 album *Live at Fillmore East.* Oakley's favorite instrument was "The Tractor," a Jazz Bass he had modified by moving the neck pickup back and installing a Guild Starfire pickup in its place. It looked odd but sounded great.

Sting played a number of different basses with the Police, including a Precision fretless. He eventually settled on a '79 Ibanez Musician fretless, making him one of the first prominent bassists to perform regularly with a Japanese-made instrument. In his post-Police years, he has returned to Fenders. He favored a '62 Jazz Bass for several years, until he came across a battered '54 Precision. "I rescued it from the orphanage about ten years ago and fell in love with its dilapidated appearance," he recalled. "There's no finish on it; it's just a wreck. Something about that really appeals to me. An old instrument is something to be cherished. I think instruments absorb and retain energy—it sounds mystical, but I really believe it."

Of all the hybrids, the most important was probably a style called "fusion"—the cross between jazz and rock (although it was closer to jazz and funk in some cases). One of the things that distinguished this style from traditional jazz was the required inclusion of an electric bass, and the consequent increase in ensemble volume.

Miles Davis generally gets credit for creating fusion on his landmark 1969 album *Bitches Brew*, which featured Dave Holland on acoustic bass and Harvey Brooks on Fender bass. Brooks was an interesting if somewhat surprising choice for the assignment. He was best known for his work with folksingers like Judy Collins and Richie Havens, and for studio work with Bob Dylan ("Like a Rolling Stone") and the team of Mike Bloomfield and Al Kooper (*Super Session*). Brooks has pointed out that his key creative influences came from Motown—"I learned by listening to James Jamerson and Bob Babbitt"—and his R&B instincts proved to be perfect for Davis's quirky improvisational schemes.

After *Bitches Brew*, Miles Davis remained committed to working with Fender bassists. His early '70s albums have some excellent work by Michael Henderson, a tremendously promising player who disappeared just as he seemed to be reaching his creative peak. In poor health, Miles himself dropped out of the music scene in 1975. When he returned six years later, he hired one of the best musicians ever to play a Fender bass— more about that in Chapter 17.

Stanley Clarke and Jaco Pastorius were the leading bassists in fusion. Jaco's predecessor in Weather Report, Alphonso Johnson, also played a key early role in establishing the electric bass in this new genre. He was

Kenny Gradney provided a funky foundation for the groove-oriented music of Little Feat, which combined elements of rock, blues, soul, country, and New Orleans R&B. Gradney joined the band just in time to cut *Dixie Chicken* in 1973. (His predecessor, Roy Estrada, was also a dedicated P-Bass man.) The band broke up after the death of founder Lowell George in 1979; they re-formed in 1988, with Gradney still on bass.

In the late '60s, the versatile Harvey Brooks used a Jazz Bass to back Bob Dylan, do session work with the Doors, and jam with Jimi Hendrix. He also cut *Super Session* with Mike Bloomfield and Al Kooper. In 1970, Brooks was invited by Miles Davis to be the Fender bassist on the seminal fusion album *Bitches Brew.*

A native of Oakland, California, Paul Jackson brought funk to fusion on Herbie Hancock's classic *Head Hunters* album in 1973. His favorite instrument at the time was a modified Telecaster Bass that had *four* Bartolini Hi-A pickups (one for each string, with an amp to match).

less flashy than Stanley and Jaco (who wasn't?) but no less solid—and he was also a fine composer whose contributions include Weather Report's "Cucumber Slumber" (*Mysterious Traveller*, 1974).

Paul Jackson was another outstanding fusion bassist, and his playing on Herbie Hancock's 1973 *Head Hunters* album (especially on their big hit, "Chameleon") was as funky as fusion ever got. And we can't consider fusion pioneers without mentioning Percy Jones of Brand X, who deserves considerable credit for forging a unique style on a '74 Precision fretless before he ever heard Jaco. Rick Laird of the original Mahavishnu Orchestra, on a Jazz Bass, also did yeoman service; his steady, structural bass lines often seemed to be the only thing holding the music together as guitarist John McLaughlin and drummer Billy Cobham traded rapid-fire outbursts. In the 1974–75 version of Mahavishnu, Ralphe Armstrong had a more featured role and soloed frequently. He played a Fender bass that was similar to Anthony Jackson's "Career Girl": it had a Precision neck on a Jazz body—but it was fretless.

Steve Swallow is an important, if often overlooked, figure in the story of the electric bass. Trained on classical piano as a child, he became an ardent jazz musician as a teenager, playing first trumpet and then acoustic bass. By the late 1960s, he had established a solid career as a straight-ahead jazz musician, working with such respected leaders as guitarist Jim Hall and saxophonist Stan Getz. And then, while strolling through a NAMM show in 1969, Swallow stopped to try out an electric bass. He abruptly dropped the upright, never to return, and since 1970 he has played electric bass—with a pick—exclusively.

Swallow's first electric bass was a Gibson EB-2. He later played several Fender and Fender-like basses (some of them semi-hollow) before obtaining a one-of-a-kind 5-string made by luthier Ken Parker in 1989. The instrument is tuned *EADGC*, and Swallow uses it with great artistry to play both impeccably solid bass lines and soaring, guitar-like solos. While he has never had the visibility (or the imitators) of Stanley Clarke or Jaco Pastorius, Swallow has been an effective champion of the electric bass, especially among jazz musicians. By playing it so well for so long, he has proven its worth.

Steve Swallow was a well-established mainstream jazz bassist when he tried out an electric bass in 1969. He abruptly quit the upright and began to play electric bass exclusively. His work is characterized by beautiful solos that are heavily influenced by his study of R&B vocalists such as Marvin Gaye and Freddie Jackson.

Chapter 17: Miles Ahead

Marcus Miller is renowned for the great sound he gets from his '77 Jazz Bass, which was modified by Roger Sadowsky. Miller "thumps" with his thumb most of the time, producing a rich, clear tone that records exceptionally well.

In addition to his work with Miles Davis, he is best known for his solo albums *The Sun Don't Lie, Tales,* and *Live & More.*

In 1980, Leo Fender left Music Man to team with two old friends, George Fullerton and Dale Hyatt, in a new company called G&L. (The "G" was for George, the "L" for Leo.) G&L offered guitars and basses that looked familiar yet incorporated new features derived from Leo's relentless trial-and-error research. The G&L L-2000 bass, for example, was available with a vibrato tailpiece and a preamp featuring three toggle switches that could be set in 18 different combinations. Not everyone thought this was progress over the elegant simplicity of the Precision Bass, but Leo explained his experiments by saying, "I owe it to musicians to make better instruments."

If Leo ever looked up from his workbench and paused to consider the progress that had been made by his Precision Bass and Jazz Bass since their introductions, he must have felt some pride. In less than 30 years, his electric basses had gained widespread acceptance and altered the course of popular music. They were in use in just about every genre of American music, from country to rock to R&B to jazz, and virtuosos like James Jamerson and Jaco Pastorius had clearly demonstrated their creative potential.

There were more virtuosos on the way. One was a young musician who was born in Brooklyn and grew up in Jamaica, Queens: Marcus Miller. Initially schooled on the clarinet, he quickly mastered several

Leo Fender started G&L in 1980. His L-2000 bass featured a Kahler vibrato tailpiece and complicated active electronics. In some ways, it was a successor to the original Jazz Bass—but was it an improvement? Some bass players thought so; others preferred his original designs.

Darryl Jones has played with Miles Davis, Sting, Madonna, Herbie Hancock, Peter Gabriel, and…oh, yes…the Rolling Stones. On the Stones' *Voodoo Lounge* tour, he favored a white '66 Jazz Bass. His bass collection also includes a '58 Precision and several Sadowskys.

The "lead bass" style of Tim Bogert in Vanilla Fudge (1967–70) was a key influence on many young players, including Jeff Berlin and Billy Shee-han. Bogert's favorite bass during his Vanilla Fudge days was a modified Precision. He later played in Cactus and then rejoined Fudge drummer Carmine Appice to back guitarist Jeff Beck.

Billy Sheehan said "old Leo Fender got it right" when he created the Precision Bass, but Billy transformed his '69 P-Bass into the homemade custom instrument he called "The Wife." It featured dual pickups (a Gibson EB-0 humbucker and a DiMarzio Model P), each with its own output jack.

Jeff Berlin improved his mid-'60s Precision Bass by having the neck cut down to Jazz Bass dimensions and installing a Badass bridge and custom-made Glen Quan pickups. In recent years, he has played Peavey and Dean basses that he helped to design; they are similar in many respects to this modified P-Bass.

While Leo Fender was creating new instruments at G&L, CBS-owned Fender was developing such curious and short-lived models as the Lead Bass, which appeared in the 1980 catalog and then vanished.

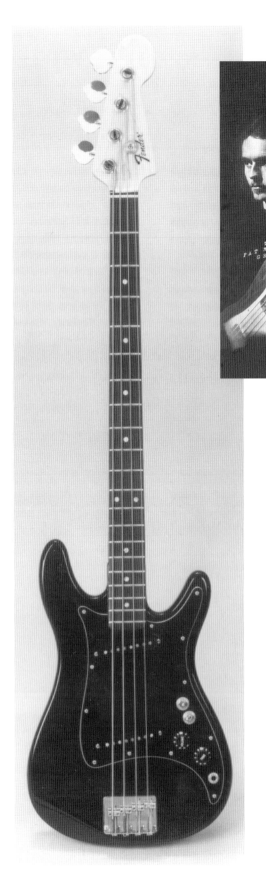

Mark Egan was the original bassist in the Pat Metheny Group, where he used a modified Precision Bass that belonged to Metheny. The blond P-Bass had a PJ pickup configuration, and Jaco Pastorius himself had removed the frets and coated the fingerboard with marine epoxy. Egan's fine playing anchored the band's stunning eponymous debut in 1978. After recording one more PMG album, *American Garage*, Mark set out on his own as a studio bassist and co-leader (with drummer Danny Gottlieb) of the group Elements.

other instruments, including electric bass. Before he was 20, Miller was working professionally as a studio bassist and jazz sideman. And then, in 1981, he got a call from Miles Davis. The famed trumpeter was coming out of retirement and putting together a new band. After a jam session at CBS Studios in New York, Miller got the nod to join the group; he played a key role on Davis's "comeback" album, *The Man with the Horn*, and a Grammy-winning 1982 live set called *We Want Miles*. A few years later, Miller collaborated with Miles as bassist-composer-arranger-producer on *Tutu*, *Amandla*, and *Siesta*.

Since high school, Miller's favorite bass had been a '77 Jazz Bass. While many mid-'70s Fender basses were mediocre instruments, noted more for their heavy wood and thick finishes than playing ease or good sound, Miller's bass was clearly the exception. On the surface, it appeared to be a fairly standard, natural-finish J-Bass with an ash body and maple neck, but it had been modified by Roger Sadowsky to improve its tone. The stock bridge was replaced by heavier Badass model, and a Stars Guitars preamp (tweaked by Sadowsky) was installed to facilitate more

Will Lee started young. This photo shows him at age 14, playing a white P-Bass with the Inner Sounds. A first-call New York studio musician since the 1980s, Will has played on well over 1,000 albums. His extensive instrument collection includes '63 Precision and Jazz Basses as well as the Sadowsky 4-string he's used for years on David Letterman's late-night TV show.

B-30

B-34

The Bullet Bass was another Fender oddity from the early '80s. It was available in short-scale and long-scale versions, although few bass players cared for either.

sophisticated tone-shaping. (In 1998, Fender offered a Marcus Miller Signature Jazz Bass that replicated the modifications.)

Miller's style combines the thumb-style playing of Larry Graham—which Marcus prefers to call "thumping," as Larry did—with the harmonic sophistication of Jaco Pastorius. Miller is noted for the clarity of his sound. "I strike the strings right in front of the chrome neck-pickup cover, not at the bottom of the neck where you get all the overtones," he told Chris Jisi. "A lot of times I don't pluck [*i.e.*, pop] at all. That developed during my jingle days, because I found that using my thumb was the best way to hear the bass coming out of a tiny TV speaker. Plus, if you use two alternating fingers, as I do when I play fingerstyle, there's always a strong note followed by a weak one; with the thumb, every note is strong."

Shortly after Miller left the Miles Davis band, his spot was taken by Darryl Jones. (Tom Barney was the interim bassist and played on one

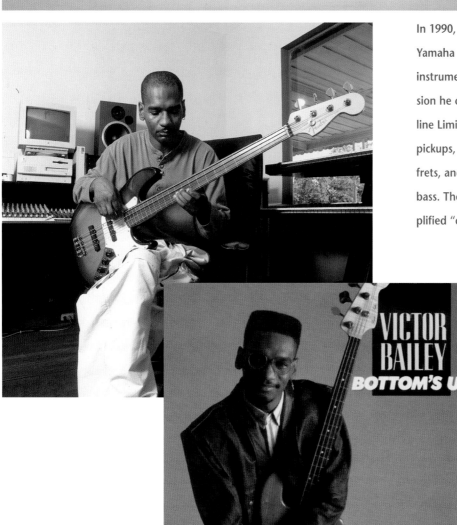

In 1990, Billy Sheehan worked with Yamaha to create the Attitude Bass, a new instrument inspired by the modified Precision he called "The Wife." The top-of-the-line Limited model had special DiMarzio pickups, a Hipshot D-tuner key, scalloped frets, and other features of Billy's Fender bass. The Deluxe (shown here) was a simplified "club musician" version.

At the age of 22, Victor Bailey had the unenviable task of succeeding Jaco in Weather Report. He did a superb job, showing he could cover Jaco's parts and bring something of his own to the music. In 1987, he released a critically acclaimed solo album, *Bottom's Up.* Throughout his career, Bailey has favored J-style basses.

In 1981, Chicago native Steve Rodby succeeded Mark Egan in the Pat Metheny Group. Although the majority of his work has been done on amplified upright, Rodby is also a master of subtle groove playing on electric bass. He has used modified Fender Precision Basses and, more recently, a Modulus 5-string.

In 1985, after seeing Anthony Jackson with his contrabass guitar, John Patitucci put his modified Jazz Bass aside and started playing a Ken Smith 6-string. He soon became one of the instrument's most distinctive players, and the most accomplished electric/acoustic doubler since Stanley Clarke.

album, *Star People*.) Jones was a Chicago native and bandmate of drummer Vince Wilburn, a nephew of Davis. He brought a funky, blues-inflected sound to two mid-'80s Davis albums, *Decoy* and *You're Under Arrest*. His approach was heavily influenced by three of the most important bassists of the '70s. "Larry Graham, Stanley Clarke, and Jaco were the key players," Jones explained. "Larry opened my ears to what the instrument could do, both sonically and technically, through slapping and popping and his use of effects like the fuzztone. Stanley broadened that concept, in terms of my thinking about soloing and developing the facility to play challenging music. Those two, in turn, allowed me to appreciate Jaco,

who expanded my focus on a more musical level. Like a lot of people at the time, my reaction to Jaco was: This isn't a bass player—this is a musician who plays bass."

After his stint with Miles, Jones joined Sting's post-Police "jazz band," where Sting eschewed bass to focus on his singing. Jones played on *The Dream of the Blue Turtles* and *Bring On the Night* and toured with the band. After various sessions and tours with Madonna and Peter Gabriel, he got a call to audition for the Rolling Stones. In 1994, he was asked to accompany the World's Greatest Rock & Roll Band as a sideman (only Mick, Keith, Charlie, and Woody are Stones). Unsurprisingly, Jones has favored vintage Fender basses for the Stones gig, including '65 and '66 Jazz Basses as well as a '58 Precision. He has also played several Fender-like basses, including a pair of Sadowsky 4-strings and an Ernie Ball Music Man Sterling (in essence, a StingRay with a J-style neck).

Darryl Jones's playing career is proof of the remarkable progress made by the Fender bass from the 1950s to the 1990s. Imagine that Bill Black had announced in 1958 he was leaving Elvis Presley to play his Precision Bass with Miles Davis. It would have been laughable. Or, even more absurdly, if Paul Chambers had told Miles he was splitting so he could go slap his bass with Elvis—not only ridiculous but unthinkable, given the racial climate of the time. Yet few people thought there was anything unusual about Darryl Jones working with both Miles Davis and the Stones. It was simply business as usual for a talented electric bassist.

Jeff, Billy & Will

Jeff Berlin is a master musician whose work has always defied categorization. A violin prodigy as a child, Berlin dropped his classical studies by the time he was 13 to focus on electric bass. (We can imagine what his parents thought.) Inspired by Jack Bruce's freewheeling approach in Cream, while still a teenager Jeff developed a style he has described as

The molten bass lines of Flea powered the Red Hot Chili Peppers to mass popularity in the late '80s. His style combines the slapping of funk with the raw power of punk and heavy metal, often delivered on a Music Man StingRay at excruciating volume.

With the Minutemen, Mike Watt fused the incredible energy of punk with powerful political commentary—often delivered in songs that lasted less than 60 seconds. His favorite instrument was a modified '68 Telecaster Bass; his favorite technique was banging the strings with his fist.

"365 notes per bar." "When I heard Jack Bruce playing with so much originality and freedom, it was a revelation. He opened my ears to improvisation and exploration, which changed my approach permanently. I wanted to find notes that other people didn't play, like Jack did."

Berlin's search for those notes led him to the Berklee College of Music, where he moved quickly from student to teacher. After two years at Berklee, he teamed up with drummer Carmine Appice, guitarist Ray Gomez, and keyboardist Steve Hill in a mid-'70s fusion band. More jazz-rock followed, including collaborations with guitarists Allan Holdsworth, John McLaughlin, and Larry Coryell. Then, in 1977, Berlin joined a band led by former Yes drummer Bill Bruford. They recorded three albums that became cult classics, including one, *Gradually Going Tornado*, that showcased Berlin's amazing facility on his modified Precision Bass. Jeff's career

Gary Willis forged a powerful style on fretless 5-string that reflected his key bass influences—Jaco, Paul Jackson, and Rocco Prestia—and his restless search for new approaches to composition and improvisation. He is best known as the co-leader, with guitarist Scott Henderson, of the fusion band Tribal Tech.

Texas bassist Tommy Shannon teamed with drummer Chris Layton in Stevie Ray Vaughan's superb backup band, Double Trouble. Shannon's favorite basses for the SRV gig included an Olympic white '62 Jazz Bass and '57 and '66 Precisions.

peaked in the mid '80s with the release of two solo albums, *Champion* and *Pump It!* The former included Berlin's version of "Dixie," the first of his amazing solo-bass renditions of famous anthems. The highlight of *Pump It!* was Berlin's note-for-note cover of Eric Clapton's guitar solo on Cream's "Crossroads," which made it clear he could play just about anything on bass—and play it with authority.

Jeff Berlin's work has always swung back and forth between rock and jazz (not to mention Latin music and several other styles), and his recordings have featured musicians from bands ranging from Journey to Chick Corea's Elektric Band. He shrugs at attempts to categorize his work and mentions a wide range of players who have influenced his bass style, from James Jamerson to Stanley Clarke to Tim Bogert of Vanilla Fudge.

Billy Sheehan is another Bogert disciple. "He was my biggest influence," Sheehan told Tom Mulhern. "He pushed me—unknowingly, with his Vanilla Fudge recordings—into being a fingerstyle player. He did things with his fingers that guys with picks just couldn't do." Like Berlin, Sheehan developed a singular, virtuosic bass style by absorbing a wide range of influences and then transcending them by finding his own original voice. A voice that, in Sheehan's case, has usually been expressed at considerable volume.

Sheehan's originality is based on both his technical innovations and his unique sound. He emerged in the late '70s with the Buffalo-based band Talas, where the spotlight was on Billy's dazzling speed, harmonics, and "hammering" technique—which invited comparisons with guitarist Eddie Van Halen. In 1984, Sheehan joined a band led by flamboyant vocalist David Lee Roth and got a chance to showcase his chops in onstage duels with guitarist Steve Vai. After he split from Roth in 1987, Sheehan put together Mr. Big, a hard rock outfit in which he had more control of the material.

The basis of Sheehan's sound—which has been described as sounding like a chain saw going through chocolate pudding—was a heavily modi-

Studio ace Lee Sklar has played on dozens of hit records and is well known for his stints with James Taylor and Phil Collins. Lee's favorite studio instrument is a modified P-Bass. The neck is from a '62 Precision; it was reshaped to J-Bass dimensions and has mandolin frets for more precise intonation.

Steve Harris of Iron Maiden is a longtime P-Bass devotee. His "Number One" bass is a '69 or '70 Precision that has been refinished several times. Praising Precisions, Harris said: "I really like the roundness on their bottom end. I can get a lot of top, real lows, the midrange, and everything—really solid."

fied Fender bass he called "The Wife." The bass started out as a '69 Precision. Because of his admiration for the "super deep" tone Yardbirds' bassist Paul Samwell-Smith got from his Gibson bass, Sheehan added a Gibson EB-0 pickup in the neck position. Not knowing how to connect two pickups to one output jack, he simply added a second jack. He replaced the Precision's neck with one from a '68 Telecaster Bass (which had the same peghead shape as the original '51 P-Bass). The stock pickup was yanked in favor of a DiMarzio Model P. A Schaller bridge and Schaller tuning machines replaced the worn-out originals. The upper frets were scalloped to facilitate string bends. Stove bolts attached a heavy-duty strap to the body. With a few more refinements and a couple of decals, Sheehan had created his own custom Fender bass.

Because of the two output jacks, Billy connected his bass to two amps, one for the low end from the EB-0 pickup and one for the brighter sound of the P-style pickup. At one point he developed this into a massive rig that included distortion preamps to fine-tune the "chainsaw" high end and huge subwoofers that reach down to the bottom of the human hearing range for the "chocolate pudding" bottom.

After years of heavy playing, "The Wife" was beginning to disintegrate, so Sheehan worked with Yamaha R&D to create a replacement. Introduced in 1990, the Attitude Limited Bass duplicated the double-output setup of the Fender hybrid and featured improvements like a strengthened neck joint and a Hipshot Xtender key, which has a lever that drops the *E* string down a half- or whole-step. (Yamaha later offered lower-priced Attitude basses that had the same basic design but fewer bells and whistles.)

In recent years Sheehan has expanded his musical horizons by performing and recording with the trio Niacin, which includes organist John Novello and former P-Funk drummer Dennis Chambers. The trio's wide-open, improvisational style is far from the hard rock bombast of the David Lee Roth band and Mr. Big, yet Sheehan's style and sound fit perfectly.

The most versatile '80s bassist of them all was Will Lee. The son of an orchestra bassist/educator (Dr. William F. Lee III of the University of Miami) and a big-band singer, Will grew up surrounded by music. After trying piano and then drums, he settled on electric bass. His first bass was a cheap Japanese instrument, but he took the money from his gigs with

In Latin music, the legendary electric bassist Sal Cuevas is renowned for an innovative approach that applied slapping and other R&B and jazz techniques. Some of his best work was on Ray Barretto's *Rican/Struction* and the Fania All-Stars' albums *Crossover* and *Rhythm Machine*.

a surf band to buy a white Precision. Will quickly mastered the instrument, and by the time he was 18 he had landed a job with a New York horn band, Dreams, succeeding his idol, Chuck Rainey.

Lee soon made a name for himself as a smart, versatile player (and singer), and by the early '80s he was one of the busiest session players in New York, cutting dozens of jingles and recording albums with everyone from the Bee Gees to the Brecker Brothers. Although much of his session work was anonymous, he landed a highly visible gig as a member of the band on David Letterman's late-night show, a spot he has held continuously for more than 25 years.

Aside from having quick ears and an encyclopedic knowledge of pop music, Lee is one of the most potent groove players of all time. "My basic approach can be summed up in two words," he told Chris Jisi. "'The pocket.' The most important function of the instrument is creating and holding down grooves." Will's knack for doing just that, often with only a few well-chosen and perfectly placed notes, is nothing less than astounding. He is quick to credit such key influences as Rainey and Willie Weeks (especially for his work on "Voices Inside (Everything Is Everything)" from *Donny Hathaway Live*), but Lee's talent in this area is almost without peer. He has taken the rhythmic innovations of Jamerson and the other early R&B greats, mixed in the melodic genius of McCartney, and then added a dash of hipness—without ever losing touch with the groove.

After using (and tinkering with) his white P-Bass for several years, Lee moved on to Jazz Basses and then to Sadowsky J-style basses. His well-worn black Sadowsky has an ash body, maple neck, and stock pickups from an early-'60s Jazz Bass ("the relationship between pickups and wood is essential, and the old Fenders just sounded better"). His sunburst TV-show bass is much the same, except for a maple top on the body. He always leaves the chrome pickup cover on his basses, finding it a useful anchor point for both finger- and pick-style playing.

The considerable skill of bassists such as Marcus Miller, Darryl Jones, Jeff Berlin, Billy Sheehan, and Will Lee made the 1980s an exciting era for bass. As great as they were, though, it was a decade of musical as well as political conservatism. The musical concepts that dominated were essentially extensions of the radical ideas of the '60s and '70s. The big question, as the 1990s approached, was: Will there be a new breakthrough?

Chapter 18: Forward Into the Past

In the early '90s, Stuart Hamm worked with the Fender Custom Shop to create a new bass model, called the Urge. The idea, according to Hamm, was to build a modern-sounding bass with the "vintage look" of the classic Fender models.

The news in the early 1990s was dominated by the conflict with Iraq, which culminated in the six-week Gulf War. It was a great triumph for President George Bush, but in 1992 he lost the presidency to an obscure Arkansas politician named Bill Clinton. Clinton, who openly admired Elvis Presley and played honking R&B saxophone, represented the ascendance of the rock & roll ethos to the highest levels of political power.

In music, the story was diversity—or, perhaps more accurately, fragmentation. Rap, which featured many recycled bass lines, was on the rise with so-called "urban" listeners and the old distinction between black and white popular music seemed to be reasserting itself (although many white teenagers embraced rap as well as rock). Concertgoers turned out in droves to see Garth Brooks, whose "modern country" bridged the gap between traditional country and the energy of rock. Jazz turned in on itself, focusing on its history (and the upright bass). The Rolling Stones and Pink Floyd had hugely successful tours—and Michael Jackson married Elvis's daughter, Lisa Marie.

In 1990, a new magazine called *Bass Player* began regular publication. (A spinoff of *Guitar Player*, it had been tested with "special edition" issues in 1988 and 1989.) Its appearance confirmed the importance of the electric bass in modern music, and the magazine quickly developed a loyal following.

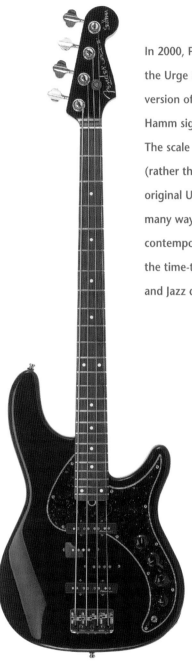

In 2000, Fender introduced the Urge II, an updated version of the original Stu Hamm signature model. The scale length is 34" (rather than the 32" of the original Urge), and in many ways it represents a contemporary hybrid of the time-tested Precision and Jazz designs.

The Kubicki Ex Factor has a lever on its "headless headstock"; by flipping the lever, a bassist can play two additional notes below open *E*. This design recalled the original concept of Jimmy Johnson, who envisioned a bass that emulated the *C*-extension of a classical upright. Johnson eventually decided a 5-string was a better idea—but his initial concept was sound.

Bass Player arrived just in time to chronicle two distinct strands in the ongoing story of the Fender bass. The first was the emergence of several new virtuosos who picked up where Jaco left off and made a case for the electric bass as a featured instrument. One of these master players was Stuart Hamm, a Berklee-trained bassist known for his work with guitarists Steve Vai and Joe Satriani as well as his solo efforts. Hamm—who had grown up listening to Chris Squire, Stanley Clarke, and Jaco—was fluent in all aspects of modern bass technique, from the most basic fingerstyle accompaniments to slapping, hammering, harmonics, and two-handed tapping. In concert, he was famous for his solo version of Vince Guaraldi's "Linus and Lucy," which demonstrated how piano-like the electric bass could be.

Early in his career, Hamm played Kubicki Factor basses almost exclusively. These sleek, headless instruments were created by luthier Phil Kubicki as a modern alternative to the traditional look and feel of Fender basses. They featured an intermediate scale length of 32" and slim necks perfect for the high-speed virtuosity of a player like Hamm. Yet their sound was solid enough to appeal to a roots-oriented bassist like Kenny Gradney of Little Feat. The Kubicki Ex Factor model had an extension on the *E* string; by flipping a lever, the bassist could play two additional fretted notes, extending the instrument's range down to *D* without sacrificing its playing ease.

In 1991–92, Hamm worked with the Fender Custom Shop to create a new bass that, he explained, "combined some of the things I like about my Kubickis with characteristics I've always associated with Fender basses, especially the warm, round sound and that great vintage look." What emerged from their collaboration was dubbed the Urge. It had a 32" scale length and custom-wound P and J pickups, along with a preamp that offered treble/mid/bass boost as well as a choice of active or passive operation. Visually, the bass was less radical than the Kubicki and had the "vintage look" Hamm craved.

The Urge proved ideal for Stuart Hamm but less so for other bassists—the scale length was the main problem—so in 2000 Fender offered a revised version called the Urge II. The new bass had a standard 34″ scale and a simplified control configuration. Reviewing it in *Bass Player*, Scott Malandrone noted that "you can clearly see the Precision and Jazz influence on the Urge II" and went on to conclude that it "takes elements of history's most popular basses and successfully combines them into a great-playing and great-sounding package."

Victor Wooten was another '90s virtuoso whose playing spanned the full range of bass technique, along with a few ideas he picked up from banjo players. Wooten burst onto the scene early in the decade as a member of Béla Fleck & the Flecktones. This unique ensemble, whose instrumental music combined elements of bluegrass, jazz, rock, R&B, and just about every other style its members had heard, was the perfect setting for Wooten's subtle mastery. He had grown up listening closely to Stanley Clarke, and he was also influenced by the two-handed tapping of guitarist Stanley Jordan. Wooten added the final ingredient while killing time on breaks during a gig at Busch Gardens in Williamsburg, Virginia. "I'd fool around with the banjo," he explained. "I'd play my regular bass patterns, but because the banjo is tuned differently, it would sound like some really outside stuff."

Wooten eventually integrated this "outside stuff" into his bass style, which features a highly developed slapping technique that combines up- and downstrokes with his right-hand thumb and left-hand hammers and pull-offs. The result is runs of astounding speed, delivered with pinpoint accuracy and an apparent ease that belies the years of work behind the technique. Wooten's playing has garnered much praise, and he continues to amaze listeners with his work with the Flecktones, in his "Bass Extremes" partnership with Steve Bailey, and on his solo albums.

Wooten, like Hamm, usually plays a 4-string. His basses are made by Fodera, and he owns several different fretted and fretless instruments based

One of the great bass virtuosos of the 1990s, Victor
Wooten developed a
unique style that combined
ideas he learned from Stanley Clarke and guitarist
Stanley Jordan with banjo
playing and a big dose of
originality. In addition to
touring and recording with
Béla Fleck & the Flecktones,
Wooten has made several
well-received solo albums.

The multi-talented Michael Manring
has an amazing style that involves
playing in a large number of alternate
tunings—and sometimes using two or
three basses at once. He has recorded
as a solo artist on Windham Hill and
Alchemy Records as well as working
with such eclectic bands as Montreux,
Sadhappy, and Cloud Chamber.

In the 1990s, many young
bassists embraced vintage
Fender instruments. Patrick
Dahlheimer of Live, shown
here with an unusual
mahogany-body '62 Preci-
sion Bass, was typical of
this group. He is an enthusiastic collector and player
of pre-CBS Fender basses.

Oteil Burbridge has emerged as one of the great bass talents on the contemporary scene, bringing his incredible melodic gift to groups as different as the Aquarium Rescue Unit and the Allman Brothers Band. Although he favors Modulus 5- and 6-string basses for his solo work and A.R.U. gigs, Oteil plays a Jazz Bass (with a pick) with the Allmans, echoing the sound of original bassist Berry Oakley.

on the company's Monarch Deluxe model. In recent years, Wooten has also played an NYC Empire bass, a Fodera-made instrument inspired by the Jazz Bass. "It's like a Fender," he explained to Bill Leigh, "and since I've never owned a Fender I've never had that sound. The bass really reminded me of Marcus [Miller] when I got it because it has a fatter tone."

The most radical bass virtuoso of the 1990s was Michael Manring. Like Hamm and Wooten, he had mastered the entire encyclopedia of bass technique, but Manring extended these devices into new sonic territory with his use of alternative tunings, ranging from simple *E*-string drops to such unusual variants as *F♯G♯AE*. He frequently changed tuning on the fly—one of his solo pieces requires "12 to 16 basic tunings and maybe a hundred tuning switches"—and his desire for maximum flexibility led to intensive instrument-development work with luthier Joe Zon. One of their creations, the Hyperbass, is a graphite-neck fretless equipped with four custom Hipshot machines and a special bridge that allows further retuning by flipping two levers. The number of possible Hyperbass tunings is mind-boggling, although Manring modestly noted in 1991, soon after the instrument debuted, that he had actually used "only about 40." (The number has since grown considerably.)

As amazing as he is as a bass technician, Manring is notable first and foremost as a composer. He emphasizes that he usually conceives his pieces away from the bass and then tries to find the right combination of tunings and techniques to execute them. This is one reason his music is so deceptive—it often sounds effortless on record, but if you see Manring play his solo pieces you realize how complicated they are. (Fellow bassist Steve Rodby, who produced Manring's *Drastic Measures* album, said his music is "almost always ten times harder than it sounds.")

It wasn't only young bassists who were infected with "vintage fever" in the '90s. Geddy Lee of Rush—a band that was formed in 1968—used his early-'70s Jazz Bass on the band's 1993 album, *Counterparts*.

During the first stage of his career, Manring used a Paul Reed Smith fretless and a Music Man StingRay fretless, which was the vehicle for many of his early retuning experiments. He also played a Japanese-made Riverhead fretted bass. After hooking up with Zon, he developed a number of specialized instruments. In addition to the Hyperbass, Manring's arsenal includes a one-of-a-kind headless fretted bass ("Vinny") as well as customized Zon Legacy Elite and Sonus basses. (Zon described the latter model, which features a slim graphite neck, as a "Jazz Bass for the '90s.") In spite of all of his custom instruments and unusual tunings, Manring remains a skillful accompanist as well as a solo artist. He has said it is very important to understand the full range of the instrument's capabilities, which are limitless: "To me, electric bass is so special, so beautiful in any context. I really

In 1982, Fender introduced its U.S. Vintage Series basses, which replicated the look and feel of the company's classic instruments. The initial offerings were '57 and '62 Precision and '62 Jazz models. (The latter was actually closer to a '60–61 J-Bass with the "stack knob" setup.) These instruments were a hit with players and foreshadowed the "back to vintage" movement of the 1990s.

believe that someday electric bass will be looked at as a really high art form."

Action & Reaction

While some artists were elevating the status of the electric bass as a solo instrument during the 1990s, a counter-revolution was taking place. With the ascendance of grunge and other forms of back-to-basics rock, the original instruments of Leo Fender enjoyed a spectacular revival. Fender Musical Instruments had serendipitously anticipated this movement with the introduction of their "Vintage Series" instruments—reproductions of classic models such as the '57 Precision and the '62 Jazz—and the bass players

In 1996, Fender rolled out the "tweaked traditional" instruments in its new Deluxe line. Shown here (L–R) are the Precision Bass Deluxe, Precision Bass Deluxe with maple finger-board, Jazz Bass Deluxe, and Jazz Bass Deluxe V. These new basses combine modern active circuitry with classic Fender design features.

of the '90s embraced these instruments as well as vintage P-Basses, J-Basses, StingRays, and even some G&L models.

A cruise through the pages of *Bass Player* during the mid to late '90s confirmed this trend. In issue after issue, young bassists were either pictured with Fender basses or quoted as using them as their main performing/recording instruments. To name just a few: Mike Mills, R.E.M. (P-Bass)…Ben Shepherd, Soundgarden (J-Bass)…Jeff Ament, Pearl Jam (StingRay, various Fender-style basses)…Sara Lee, Gang Of Four, B-52s (G&L L-2000)…John Doe, X (P-Bass)…Aimee Man (P-Bass)…Matt Malley, Counting Crows (StingRay)…Tim Cross, Sponge (P-Bass)…Bardi Martin, Candle-box (StingRay)…Matt Freeman, Rancid (J-Bass)…Melissa Auf der Maur, Hole (P-Bass)…Andrew Levy, Brand New Heavies (StingRay, P-Bass)

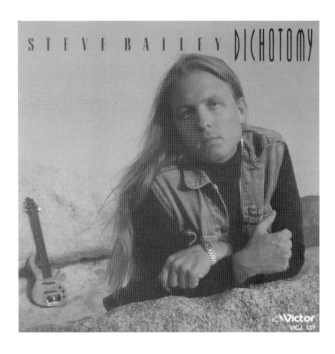

Steve Bailey emerged as an important talent in the early 1990s, displaying dazzling technique on a Heartfield DR6 fretless, a Japanese-made 6-string that Fender distributed. After a NAMM jam, he formed the duo Bass Extremes with Victor Wooten.

…Rachel Haden, That Dog (P-Bass)…Corey Parks, Nashville Pussy (J-Bass) …Drew Miller, Boiled In Lead (J-Bass)…and so on.

Typical of this movement was Patrick Dahlheimer of Live, who explained to Scott Malandrone that he had converted from modern high-tech basses to vintage Fenders after finding a '62 Precision in a pawnshop: "I bought the bass and started playing it onstage. The sound was amazing; it was *musical*. The tone didn't depend on a battery or active electronics. It was a hunk of wood and *you* had to make it work." Many of his compatriots echoed this sentiment of feeling a special connection with vintage Fender basses.

Perhaps even more telling were the veteran players who had moved (or moved back) to Fender basses. Geddy Lee of Rush, known for his "high tech" sound on Rickenbacker, Steinberger, and Wal basses, picked up his old Jazz Bass to record the album *Counterparts*. Pino Palladino adopted a '63 Precision (with flatwound strings) to record with D'Angelo. Jazz virtuoso Jimmy Earl, a devoted 6-stringer, began to play his '65 Jazz Bass again. Studio ace Randy Jackson dropped his modern 5-strings for a Fender-style bass made by Mike Lull. And Gene Perez kicked up the sound of Masters At Work remixes with a '78 Jazz Bass.

Roscoe Beck collaborated with the Fender Custom Shop on the design of a signature bass inspired by the Jazz Basses of the 1960s. It has proven to be one of the company's most successful 5-string models, uniting contemporary construction with the classic J-Bass sound.

There may have been no breakthrough players like James Jamerson or Jaco Pastorius in the 1990s—and perhaps bass playing has matured to the point that there never will be again—but as the 50th anniversary of the Precision Bass approached, Fender basses continued to exert a powerful influence. Not every great player used a Fender or Fender-like bass, but Leo Fender's original creation can legitimately be seen as the forebear of nearly all of the electric bass guitars on the market today. Just about every bass player, it seems, still has to consider the Precision Bass or Jazz Bass at some point in his or her career, and then decide whether to embrace the original instrument or choose an alternative. And instrument builders are still faced with the primacy of Leo Fender's design. At a 1996 roundtable discussion with 14 well-known bass makers, Michael Tobias opened the session by asking: "Is the Fender bass still the standard?" The builders all had different reactions to the question, but in the end one conclusion was inescapable: the instruments of Leo Fender had had a profound and enduring impact.

Finale

In *Instruments of Desire*, the prize-winning American Studies scholar (and guitarist) Steve Waksman explains the thinking of French musicologist Jacques Attali. "Instruments play a key part in his larger effort to theorize the role of music as a prophetic social force," writes Waksman, "one that contains within it the principles of cultural, economic, and political power. In the first chapter of his book, *Noise*, Attali outlines his inquiry in terms that make manifest his overarching belief in the capacity of music to embody and, indeed, herald the social order." Waksman goes on to demonstrate how musical instruments can function as "tools of social and cultural (as well as aesthetic) transformation."

Leo Fender might have been befuddled by all this talk about over arching beliefs, but he knew his electric bass was important. In 1994, former Fender executive Forrest White, who had worked closely with Leo during the company's glory years, wrote: "Today the Precision Bass is the most widely used electric bass throughout the world. I personally think it was Leo's greatest overall contribution to music, and I believe he, too, thought it was his greatest accomplishment."

It was indeed an extraordinary accomplishment. The Fender bass has proven to be a powerful force in the evolution of popular music, and as such has served as a tool of "social and cultural (as well as aesthetic) transformation." This did not happen overnight. The Precision Bass was greeted with little enthusiasm and gained limited acceptance at first. Only a few P-Basses were sold in the early 1950s, but the market was promising enough for the company to continue to produce (and improve) the instrument. By 1960, Leo Fender had created a new model, the Jazz Bass, and other companies such as Gibson, Rickenbacker, and Danelectro had entered the burgeoning bass market.

During the 1960s, the primordial sound of early rock & roll was tranformed into something much more potent and influential. The power of the electric bass, in the hands of such innovators as James Jamerson and Paul McCartney, was critical in this transformation. And rock music was no longer just a diversion; it was, as Christopher Porterfield of *Time* put it, the language of a new generation determined to usher in sweeping social change.

It may seem simplistic to ascribe social change to the invention of a musical instrument, but the line of causality is clear: without the Fender bass, rock music as we now know it was simply not possible. (Remember what Keith Richards said: "It suddenly changed…[and] I realized…it was because of the *bass*.") Rock was a powerful unifying force in the '60s, and by the end of that cataclysmic decade it dominated popular culture. In the 1970s, the influence of music featuring the Fender bass spread even further, and we were introduced to higher levels of virtuosity. When Jaco's first solo album was released in 1976, Leo Fender's "crazy" invention was firmly established as a vehicle for profound musical expression.

By the late '70s and early '80s, the importance of the electric bass was firmly established, and it proliferated in a variety of forms. A few, like the Steinberger bass, owed little to Leo Fender's designs. Nonetheless, the influence of the original Precision Bass runs through the history of the electric bass like the theme of a great symphony. It is a reference point that cannot be ignored. After dozens of competitive instruments had appeared on the market, Fender basses still remained of prime importance. Even for the players who eventually chose *not* to use them, they were so dominant that they demanded consideration. And they have endured.

If it's unsurprising that James Jamerson chose a Precision Bass in 1961—because there were so few alternatives—then it's quite telling that Patrick Dahlheimer chose one in 1998, when there were so *many* alternatives. In an industry where the flavor of the month is always changing, Fender basses have remained a constant. Their sound has forever altered the way popular music is written and played, and that music has had a profound effect on the everyday lives of countless people around the world.

Sources

During my tenure as Editor of *Bass Player* (1989–96), we published many articles that touched upon the history of the electric bass, and I began to accumulate files drawn from a variety of sources: magazines, newspapers, books, liner notes, videos, radio programs, and the World Wide Web. I also interviewed and spoke informally with many musicians and music writers about different aspects of the instrument's development. The following articles and books were helpful in preparing this book, and many of them are quoted in the text:

Articles

Ashton, Adrian. "Bring It on Home: The John Paul Jones Interview." *Bass Player*, November 1994.

Bacon, Tony. "Steve Harris—Iron Maiden." *Bass Player*, October 1992.

____ . "Paul McCartney: Meet the Beatle." *Bass Player*, July/Aug 1995.

Bass Player staff (Jim Roberts, Karl Coryat, Chris Jisi). "Masters of Funk." *Bass Player*, September 1992.

Blecha, Peter. "Discovered! The World's First Electric Bass Guitar." *Vintage Guitar*, March 1999.

Brown, G. "Carol Kaye." *Bass Player*, Jan/Feb 1993.

Conrow, Ray. "In Memory of Berry Oakley." *Bass Player*, Jan/Feb 1993.

Coryat, Karl. "Flea Jumps in a Different Direction." *Bass Player*, Jan/Feb 1992.

____ . "Stanley Clarke Scores Big." *Bass Player*, Sept/Oct 1993.

____ . "Geddy Lee: Still Going!" *Bass Player*, December 1993.

PRECISION BASS

The new four string Precision Bass is one of the most revolutionary instruments to make an appearance in many years. It is the answer to every bass player's desire for a portable instrument of extremely fine tone quality, plus playing ease and comfort. This remarkable new instrument is infinitely easier to play than a conventional bass, inasmuch as the technique is like that used in playing a guitar. Very little string action is required to obtain full rich bass volume, thereby eliminating the effort that went in to playing the old style bass.

The neck of this instrument is slender and fretted, and the string adjustment is close to the frets, thus enabling the player to play with greatly increased speed. Most players find that their technique improves very rapidly with the use of this new instrument and that they can play considerably more difficult work than ever before.

With the Precision Bass it is possible to obtain considerably more volume than with a conventional instrument. The space required for storage or carrying of this instrument is approximately ⅓ of that required for the old type bass.

The Fender Precision Bass opens an entirely new field of bass playing, and already they have become stock items in a great many of the nation's top musical organizations.

Available as an accessory is a fine molded plush lined case, covered in Dupont "Grain Hair Seal," or a padded plastic leather bag.

LIONEL HAMPTON

____ . "Sting: Bring on the Note." *Bass Player*, March 2000.

____ . "Phil Lesh." *Bass Player*, June 2000 and July 2000.

Crisafulli, Chuck. "Duck Dunn: He's a Soul Man." *Bass Player*, December 1994.

Dr. Licks (Allan Slutsky) with James Jamerson Jr. "James Jamerson: Interview with the Ghost of Studio A." *Bass Player*, Spring 1990.

____ . "Who Is Bob Babbitt and How Did He Get All Those Gold Records?" *Bass Player*, March 1994.

DuClos, Michael. "Carl Thompson: Veteran Bassbuilder with Vision." *Bass Player*, February 1996.

Feather, Leonard. "Hamp-lified Fiddle May Lighten Bassists' Burdens." *Down Beat*, July 30, 1952.

Forte, Dan. "The Ventures: Still Rockin' After All These Years." *Guitar Player*, September 1981.

Garbarini, Vic. "Sting." *Bass Player*, April 1992.

Gerety, Sean. "Percy Jones." *Bass Player*, October 1992.

Green, Tony. "Larry Graham." *Bass Player*, September 1996.

Gruhn, George. "Gibson Upright Electric Bass." *VG Classics*, June 1997.

Hicks, David. "Vintage Volume: The Great Bass Amps of the '60s." *Bass Player*, July/Aug 1992.

Isola, Gregory. "Little Feat's Kenny Gradney." *Bass Player*, December 1995.

____ . "Bill Wyman: Back & Blue." *Bass Player*, May 1998.

Jansson, Mikael. "I Go Pogo: A Brief History of the Electric Upright Bass." 1994 *Bass Buyer's Guide* (*Bass Player* special issue).

____ and Scott Malandrone. "Jurassic Basses: Was There Electric Bass Before Leo?" *Bass Player*, July 1997.

____ . "Paul Jackson: A Headhunter Speaks." *Bass Player*, March 1998.

____ . "Totally Weird Basses: Regal's Bassoguitar." *Bass Player*, February 1999.

____ . "Totally Weird Basses: The Stroh Bass." *Bass Player*, September 1999.

Jisi, Chris. "The Anthony Jackson Interview." *Bass Player*, Spring 1990 and Summer 1990.

____ . "Will Lee." *Bass Player*, Fall 1990.

____ . "Pino Palladino: Fretless Magician." *Bass Player*, March 1992.

____ . "Alphonso Johnson: Fusion Revolutionary." *Bass Player*, April 1992.

____ with Anthony Jackson. "Joe Osborn: The Saga of a Studio Pioneer." *Bass Player*, May/June 1992.

_____ . "Marcus Miller." *Bass Player*, October 1992.

_____ . "The Big Groove of Gary Willis." *Bass Player*, April 1993.

_____ with Anthony Jackson and Dan Schwartz. "The Heroic Bass of Jack Casady." *Bass Player*, Sept/Oct 1993.

_____ . "Max Bennett." *Bass Player*, November 1994.

_____ . "Chris Squire Talks About *Talk*." *Bass Player*, November 1994.

_____ . "Darryl Jones: Like a Rolling Stone." *Bass Player*, Jan/Feb 1995.

_____ . "John Entwistle: Return of the Ox." *Bass Player*, April 1996.

_____ . "Groove Convergence! Will Lee Interviews Chuck Rainey." *Bass Player*, February 1997.

_____ . "Oteil Burbridge Breaks Out." *Bass Player*, August 1997.

_____ . "Double Trouble: Roscoe Beck Interviews Tommy Shannon." *Bass Player*, November 1997.

_____ . "Francis Rocco Prestia." *Bass Player*, December 1997.

_____ . "Jeff Berlin: The Return of a Player." *Bass Player*, January 1998.

_____ . "Gene Perez Is in the House!" *Bass Player*, July 1999.

_____ . "New York Soul Stew: The Legendary Jerry Jemmott." *Bass Player*, October 1999.

Johnston, Richard. "David Hungate: Studio Ace." *Bass Player*, March 1992.

Kohman, Peter Stuart. "Surf Bass: Out of the Doghouse." *Vintage Guitar*, May 1997.

Leigh, Bill. "Flecktone Alone: Victor Wooten Arrives as a Solo Artist." *Bass Player*, February 1998.

Malandrone, Scott. "The Ampeg Story." *Bass Player*, March 1995.

_____ . "Billy Sheehan: Bare Bones Bass with Mr. Big." *Bass Player*, April 1996.

_____ . "Patrick Dahlheimer: Live Stock." *Bass Player*, July 1997.

_____ . "Fender Stu Hamm Urge II" (product review). *Bass Player*, June 2000.

Martin, Bill. "Chris Squire: Creating a New Dimension." *Bass Player*, November 1994.

Milkowski, Bill. "Portrait of Jaco," *Bass Player*, Jan/Feb 1991.

_____ . "Victor Wooten: Bass Ace of the Flecktones." *Bass Player*, Jan/Feb 1991.

_____ . "George Porter Jr.: Funkmaster." *Bass Player*, April 1996.

_____ . "Life After Jaco." *Bass Player*, September 1997.

_____ . "Blues Legend Dave Myers." *Bass Player*, December 1998.

Murphy, Bill. "Bass Culture: Dub Reggae's Low-End Legacy." *Bass Player*, November 1996.

Newman, Mike. "Monk Montgomery: The First Man to Record on Bass Guitar." *Guitar Player*, September 1977.

Roberts, Jim. "Steve Swallow." *Guitar Player*, November 1987.

____ . "Steve Rodby." *Guitar Player*, December 1987.

____ . "Verdine White." *Guitar Player*, October 1988.

____ . "Victor Bailey." *Guitar Player*, July 1989.

____ . "Billy Sheehan: Power & Precision." *Bass Player*, Spring 1990.

____ . "Harvey Brooks: A Long Time Comin'...Back." *Bass Player*, March/April 1991.

____ . "Good Times, Bad Times: Bill Wyman Chronicles the Rise of the Rolling Stones." *Bass Player*, May/June 1991.

____ . "Michael Manring's Drastic Measures." *Bass Player*, May/June 1991.

____ . "Stuart Hamm: He's Got the Urge." *Bass Player*, July/Aug 1991.

____ and Chris Jisi. "Free-Floating Fretless: Mark Egan." *Bass Player*, Jan/Feb 1992.

____ . "Dancing in the Dark: An Interview with Steve Swallow." *Bass Player*, May/June 1992.

____ . "The Stuart Hamm Signature Bass." *Bass Player*, September 1992.

____ . "Jack Bruce: Renaissance Man." *Bass Player*, Sept/Oct 1993.

____ . "Michael Manring Rocks!" *Bass Player*, Jan/Feb 1994.

____ . "Pushing the Envelope: A Bassmakers Roundtable." *Bass Player*, January 1996.

Sievert, Jon. "Michael Rhodes" (Tommy Cogbill sidebar). *Bass Player*, September 1992.

Sklarevski, Alexis. "Lee Sklar: Interview with a Studio Legend." *Bass Player*, Jan/Feb 1992.

Smith, Richard R. "Classic Fender Basses." *Guitar Player*, March 1989.

____ . "The Fender Precision Bass—A Classic: 1952–1964." *Bass Player*, Spring 1990.

____ . "Leo Fender's Bass Revolution." *Bass Player*, September 1996.

Snowden, Don. "Bernard Edwards." *Bass Player*, September 1992.

____ . "Robbie Shakespeare." *Bass Player*, Jan/Feb 1993.

Teagle, John. "Fender Myth Debunked! (Part I)." *Vintage Guitar*, March 1999.

Wheeler, Tom. "Keith Richards." *Guitar Player*, December 1989.

Books

Bacon, Tony. *The Ultimate Guitar Book*. New York: Alfred A. Knopf, 1991.

____ and Paul Day. *The Fender Book: A Complete History of Fender Electric Guitars*. San Francisco: GPI/Miller Freeman, 1992.

____ and Barry Moorhouse. *The Bass Book: A Complete Illustrated History of Bass Guitars*. San Francisco: GPI/Miller Freeman, 1995.

Blasquiz, Klaus. *The Fender Bass*. Milwaukee: Hal Leonard Publishing, 1990.

Brun, Paul. *A History of the Double Bass*. France: self-published, 1989.

Dr. Licks (Allan Slutsky). *Standing in the Shadows of Motown: The Life and Times of Legendary Bassist James Jamerson*. Milwaukee: Hal Leonard Publishing, 1989.

George, Nelson. *The Death of Rhythm & Blues*. New York: E.P. Dutton, 1989.

Gleick, James. *Chaos: Making a New Science*. New York: Viking, 1987.

Gruhn, George and Walter Carter. *Electric Guitars & Basses: A Photographic History*. San Francisco: Miller Freeman, 1994.

____ . *Gruhn's Guide to Vintage Guitars*. San Francisco: Miller Freeman, 1999.

Guralnick, Peter. *Last Train to Memphis: The Rise of Elvis Presley*. Boston: Little, Brown & Company, 1994.

Hopkins, Gregg and Bill Moore. *Ampeg: The Story Behind the Sound*. Milwaukee: Hal Leonard Publishing, 1999.

Massey, Howard. *Behind the Glass: Top Record Producers Tell How They Craft the Hits*. San Francisco: Miller Freeman, 2000.

Milkowski, Bill. *Jaco: The Extraordinary and Tragic Life of Jaco Pastorius*. San Francisco: Miller Freeman, 1995.

Mulhern, Tom, ed. *Bass Heroes: 30 Great Bass Players*. San Francisco: GPI/Miller Freeman, 1993.

Nichols, Geoff. *The Drum Book: A History of the Rock Drum Kit*. San Francisco: Miller Freeman, 1997.

Planyavsky, Alfred. *The Baroque Double Bass Violone*. Lanham, MD & London: Scarecrow Press, 1998.

Smith, Richard R. *Fender: The Sound Heard 'round the World*. Fullerton, CA: Garfish Publishing, 1995.

Trynka, Paul, ed. *Rock Hardware: 40 Years of Rock Instrumentation*. San Francisco: Miller Freeman, 1996.

Waksman, Steve. *Instruments of Desire: The Electric Guitar and the Shaping of Musical Experience*. Cambridge, MA: Harvard University Press, 1999.

Ward, Ed with Geoffrey Stokes and Ken Tucker. *Rock of Ages: The Rolling Stone History of Rock*. New York: Rolling Stone Press/Summit Books, 1986.

Wheeler, Tom. *American Guitars: An Illustrated History*. New York: Harper-Collins, 1992.

Whitburn, Joel. *Billboard Top 100 Singles: 1955–1992*. Milwaukee: Hal Leonard Publishing, 1993.

White, Forrest. *Fender: The Inside Story*. San Francisco: GPI/Miller Freeman, 1994.

p. 11, Marcus Miller, by Karjean Ng

p. 15, Fender Factory 1952, from the collection of Richard Smith

p. 22, Regal Bassoguitar, from the collection of Richard Smith

p. 23, Dobro Upright Bass, from the collection of Richard Smith

p. 24, Gibson Upright Bass, by Experience Music

p. 26, Regal Electric Upright, from the collection of Richard Smith

p. 27, Vega Electric Upright, from the collection of Richard Smith

p. 29, Audiovox Model 736, by Experience Music

p. 31, Design Patent for Orig. P-bass, from the collection of Richard Smith

p. 32, Orig. Precision bass, by John Peden

p. 36, Fender ad for P-bass/Bassman amp, from the collection of Richard Smith

p. 37, Monk Montgomery, from the collection of Richard Smith

p. 38, Shifte Henri, from the collection of Tom Wheeler

p. 39, Rickenbacker "Frying Pan", from the collection of Richard Smith

p. 40, "Butterfly Bass" graphic, by John Peden/Paul Haggard

p. 41, Early Drum set, courtesy of Balafon Books

p. 42, Close-up of '55 pick-up, from the collection of Richard Smith

p. 44, '55 Precision bass, by John Peden

p. 44, '55 Precision bass w/ amp, from the collection of Richard Smith

p. 45, '57 Precision bass, by John Peden

p. 46, Close-up of a split-coil pickup, from the collection of Richard Smith

p. 47, Bill Black, Michael Ochs Archives

p. 49, Dave Myers, courtesy of Dave Myers

p. 53, Danelectro Long Horn 6, courtesy of Balafon Books

p. 53, Rickenbacker 4000, courtesy of Balafon Books

p. 57, Custom-color Fender basses, from the collection of Richard Smith

p. 61, Joe Osborn, by Ebet Roberts

p. 62, Jazz Bass prototype, from the collection of Richard Smith

p. 62, Jazz Bass prototype pickup, from the collection of Richard Smith

p. 63, Early Jazz bass w/ stacked knobs, courtesy of John Slog

p. 64, Fender Bass VI, '61, from the collection of Richard Smith

p. 65, Max Bennett, courtesy of Max Bennett

p. 68, "St. James" graphic, Created by Paul Haggard

p. 69, Jamerson & The Funk Machine, by Jon Sievert

p. 69, Fender Bass V, courtesy of Balafon Books

p. 70, Chuck Rainey, courtesy of Chuck Rainey

p. 73, Memphis Boys, by Dan Penn

p. 74, Jerry Jemmott, courtesy of Jerry Jemmott

p. 75, David Hood, courtesy David Hood

p. 77, Bob Babbitt, by Rick Malkin

p. 78, Paul McCartney w/Hofner 500/1, Pictorial Press

p. 80, Paul McCartney w/ Rick. 4001S, Pictorial Press

p. 85, John Paul Jones, by Neil Zlozower

p. 86, John Entwistle, by Len DeLessio

p. 88, Chris Squire, by Neil Zlozower

p. 92, Jack Casady w/ Jazz Bass, Redferns

p. 93, Jack Casady w/ a modified Guild, courtesy of Jack Casady

p. 94, Fender Bassman amp, from the collection of Richard Smith

p. 95, Jack Casady w/ a Versatone amp, courtesy of Jack Casady

p. 96, Phil Lesh, by Jay Blakesberg

p. 106, Jack Bruce w/ Fender Bass VI, Redferns

p. 107, Jack Bruce w/ Gibson EB-3, Redferns

p. 108, Gibson Electric Bass, by John Peden

p. 109, Gibson EB-2, courtesy of Balafon Books

p. 113, Bootsy Collins w/ star bass, by Paul Natkin

p. 115, Larry Graham, Redferns

p. 117, Rocco Prestia, courtesy of Rocco Prestia

p. 119, Music Man StingRay, from the collection of Richard Smith

p. 120, Verdine White, courtesy of Verdine White

p. 123, Jaco w/ fretted bass, by Richard Sassaman

p 124, Jaco w/ fretless, by Tom Copi

p. 125, Ampeg AUB-1 fretless, by Evan Sheeley

p. 128, Pino Palladino, by Paul Natkin

p. 132, Anthony Jackson, by Ebet Roberts

p. 133, Jimmy Johnson, by Margo Reyes

p. 137, Early Modulus Graphite bass, by Geoff Gould

p. 139, Tony Levin, courtesy of Tony Levin

p. 141, Sid Vicious, by Ebet Roberts

p. 142, Aston "Family Man" Barrett, by Peter Simon

p. 143, Robbie Shakespeare, by Ebet Roberts

p. 145, Sting, by Steve Jennings

p. 146, Berry Oakley, ABB Archives

p. 147, Kenny Gradney, Michael Ochs Archives

p. 149, Steve Swallow, by Ebet Roberts

p. 151, G&L L-2000 bass, from the collection of Richard Smith

p. 152, Darryl Jones, by Neil Zlozower

p. 152, Tim Bogert, courtesy of Tim Bogert

p. 153, Billy Sheehan, by Neil Zlozower

p. 153, Jeff Berlin, by Neil Zlozower

p. 154, Mark Egan, courtesy of Mark Egan

p. 155, Will Lee, courtesy of Will Lee

p. 157, Victor Bailey, courtesy of Fender

p. 158, Steve Rodby, by Paul Natkin

p. 158, John Patitucci, by Neil Zlozower

p. 160, Flea, by Jay Blakesberg

p. 161, Gary Willis, courtesy of Gary Willis

p. 163, Lee Sklar, courtesy of Lee Sklar

p. 164, Steve Harris, by Neil Zlozower

p. 165, Sal Cuevas, by Dan Thress

p. 168, Stuart Hamm, courtesy of Fender

p. 169, Kubicki Ex Factor, courtesy of Balafon Books

p. 172, Victor Wooten, by Rick Malkin

p. 174, Oteil Burbridge, courtesy of Modulus Guitars

p. 175, Geddy Lee, by Neil Zlozower

p. 179, Roscoe Beck, by Max Crace

p. 183, Fender Catalog, 1954, from the collection of Richard Smith

p. 184, Fender Catalog, 1955, from the collection of Richard Smith

p. 185, Fender Catalog, 1958, from the collection of Richard Smith

p. 188, Fender Catalog, 1961, from the collection of Richard Smith

The Lowdown On Bass

Bass Player gives you the tools you need to be a better bassist. All of our writers and editors are working musicians and teachers——with years of experience onstage and in the studio. We're connected to the players and equipment gurus who make things happen in the bass world and you can be too. For artist features, lessons, and gear reviews designed by players for players, check us out at www.bassplayer.com.

To Subscribe:
(800) 234-1831 or www.bassplayer.com

THE MUSIC PLAYER NETWORK

a division of
United Entertainment Media
... networking the future

WHEN IT COMES TO THE BASS, WE WROTE THE BOOK.

The Bass Player Book
Equipment, Technique, Styles,
and Artists
Edited by Karl Coryat

Whether you're a novice or
seasoned bassist, play acoustic or
electric, you'll find instruction and
inspiration here. This all-in-one
handbook covers theory,
positioning, groove, slap,
harmonics and more, providing in-
depth musical examples in all key styles. You get experts'
advice on choosing equipment, plus personal insights
from Paul McCartney, Stanley Clarke, Les Claypool, and
other bass innovators.
Softcover, 224 pages, ISBN 0-87930-573-8, $22.95

Bass Heroes
Styles, Stories & Secrets of 30
Great Bass Players
Edited by Tom Mulhern

Thirty of the world's greatest bass
players in rock, jazz, pop, blues,
and funk share their musical
influences, playing techniques, and
personal opinions in this collection
of firsthand interviews. You'll hear
from John Entwistle, Bill Wyman,
John Patitucci, Marcus Miller, Carol Kaye, Chuck Rainey,
Larry Graham, Bootsy Collins, and many more.
Softcover, 201 pages, ISBN 0-87930-274-7, $17.95

The Bass Book
A Complete Illustrated History
of Bass Guitars
By Tony Bacon and Barry
Moorhouse

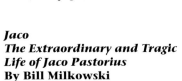

Based on interviews with electric
bass designers and makers, this
book celebrates one of the 20th
century's most significant
inventions and its impact. From
the birth of the bass in 1951 through the mid-'90s, rich
color photos bring you up close with rare, classic, and
modern models from Alembic, Fender, Gibson,
Rickenbacker, and others.
Cloth, 108 pages, ISBN 0-87930-368-9, $22.95

Studio Bass Masters
Session Tips & Techniques from
Top Bass Players
By Keith Rosiér; Foreword by
Don Was

Eleven top electric and upright
session bassists reveal their secrets
of success in this enlightening and
practical book/CD set. Session aces
like Leland Sklar and Hutch
Hutchinson discuss recording experiences, studio
techniques, styles and chops, favorite basses, set ups, and
more. The CD provides basslines from each player,
illustrating diverse musical styles.
Softcover with CD, 116 pages, ISBN 0-87930-558-4, $19.95

Jaco
The Extraordinary and Tragic
Life of Jaco Pastorius
By Bill Milkowski

This biography has become the classic
portrait of the troubled genius who
revolutionized modern electric bass.
Featuring reminiscences from artists
who played with him, it reveals how
Jaco played melodies, chords,
harmonics and percussive effects
simultaneously, while fusing jazz, classical, R&B, rock,
reggae, pop, and punk—all before age 35, when he met
his tragic death.
Softcover, 263 pages, ISBN 0-87930-426-X, $14.95

The Working Bassist's Tool Kit
The Art and Craft of Successful
Bass Playing
By Ed Friedland

Whether you're just starting out or
already working, this book/CD set
is your ultimate guide to successful
gigs in rock, jazz, blues, R&B, and
more. You'll learn key skills for
going pro, techniques for staying
hot, and tips for tackling any gig—
electric or acoustic. Packed with musical examples and
exercises.
Softcover with CD, 120 pages, ISBN 0-87930-615-7, $19.95

(Formerly Miller Freeman Books)

AVAILABLE AT FINE BOOK AND MUSIC STORES EVERYWHERE.
OR CONTACT:

6600 Silacci Way • Gilroy, CA 95020 USA
Phone: Toll free (866) 222-5232 • Fax: (408) 848-5784
E-mail: backbeat@rushorder.com • **Web:** www.backbeatbooks.com